FANTASTIC
furniture

Intriguing Paint Techniques & Projects

FANTASTIC
furniture

Intriguing Paint Techniques & Projects

By Mickey Baskett

Sterling Publishing Co., Inc.
New York

Prolific Impressions Production Staff:

Editor: Mickey Baskett
Copy: Phyllis Mueller
Graphics: Dianne Miller, Michael Moore
Photography: Greg Wright, Jerry Mucklow
Administrative: Jim Baskett
Styling: Laney McClure

Acknowledgements

Mickey Baskett thanks the following for their generous contributions:

Plaid Enterprises, Inc.
1649 International Blvd.
P.O. Box 7600
Norcross, Georgia, U.S.A.
For supplying artists with painting products such as FolkArt® acrylic paints; FolkArt® varnishes; Decorator Products® Glazes, Tools, and Stamps; Durable Colors™ indoor/outdoor paints; and Apple Barrel® indoor/outdoor acrylic paints.

The artists who contributed their talents to this book. *The following talented people made this book possible: Stephanie Corder, Ginger Edwards, Kathi Malarchuk, Jeff McWilliams, Gigi Smith-Burns, Allison Stilwell, Tracy Page Stilwell, and Chris Stokes. Each of these gifted artists has her own unmistakable style, making each piece of furniture unique. When all the projects are combined in this book it makes for a fantastic collection. I thank you all for sharing your talent.*

Library of Congress Cataloging-in-Publication Data Available

Published by Sterling Publishing Company, Inc.
387 Park Avenue South, New York, NY 10016

Produced by Prolific Impressions, Inc.
160 South Candler St., Decatur, GA 30030
© 1999 by Prolific Impressions, Inc.

Distributed in Canada by Sterling Publishing
c/o Canadian Manda Group, One Atlantic Avenue, Suite 105
Toronto, Ontario, Canada M6K 3E7
Distributed in Great Britain and Europe by Cassell PLC
Wellington House, 125 Strand, London WC2R 0BB, England
Distributed in Australia by Capricorn Link (Australia) Pty. Ltd.
P.O. Box 6651, Baulkham Hills, Business Centre, NSW 2153 Australia

Printed in the United States
All rights reserved.

ISBN 0-8069-6263-1

CONTENTS

CREATE FANTASTIC FURNITURE — FAST

With paint, you can give new life to old furniture or transform inexpensive, unfinished pieces into fantastic works of art that you'll enjoy for years. Painting furniture and using furniture pieces you decorated yourself are rewarding and creative ways to add personal touches to the rooms of your home. The projects in this book are examples of the many techniques you can use to decorate furniture:

- *Color block painting*
- *Stenciling*
- *Stamping*
- *Stippling*
- *Sponging*
- *Glazing*
- *Distressing*
- *Design painting*

They are easy to accomplish and inexpensive to complete. Step-by-step instructions, numerous photographs, and patterns are provided.

These Practical Pieces Will Add Style to Your Rooms.

A wide assortment of furniture types and styles—old and new and in-between, fanciful and formal, large and small are represented in these projects—yet each is very practical and useable, showcasing the versatility and functionality of painted furniture. The designs can be adapted to fit a variety of furniture pieces and for multiple uses. You may even have pieces around your house that would benefit from a little paint. Use the ideas, techniques, and motifs presented here to create your own inspired treasures, choosing colors to suit your decor and color schemes. The finished results will express your style, enliven your rooms, and earn admiration and compliments from your family and friends. ❧

SUPPLIES

for furniture preparation & base painting

For Cleaning & Stripping

Mild Detergent or Bubble Bath:

If you are going to colorfully paint your piece of furniture, you will find that stripping is not necessary—just clean it up. To remove dirt, dust, cobwebs, etc, clean it with a cleaner that does not leave a gritty residue. Effective cleaners include mild dishwashing detergent and bubble bath. Mix the cleaner with water and wash the furniture with a cellulose sponge. Rinse and wipe dry with soft cloth rags.

Paint Thinner:

Use paint thinner and a **steel wool pad** to remove waxy buildup on wood stained pieces and old varnish or shellac.

Paint Stripper:

There are several reasons you may wish to strip the old furniture piece. If you plan to stain, pickle, or color wash the piece, then you will need to get down to the bare wood. Also, if the piece of furniture is covered with layers of badly flaking, wrinkled or uneven paint that can't be just sanded smooth, stripping is necessary. There are many brands of paint strippers available in do-it-yourself or hardware stores. Apply **paint stripper** with a brush. When the paint begins to wrinkle and lift, remove with a **paint scraper**.

For Sanding & Filling

Sandpaper:

Sandpaper is available in different grits for different types of sanding. Generally, start with medium grit sandpaper and then use fine grit to sand before painting. Between coats of paint, sand lightly with fine or extra fine sandpaper.

Sanding Block:

This is a wooden block that sandpaper is wrapped around and aids smooth sanding on flat surfaces.

Electric Sander:

A handheld, electric finishing sander aids in sanding large, flat areas. Use wet/dry sandpaper and wet it to keep down dust. Wipe away sanding dust with a **tack cloth**.

Wood Filler:

Wood filler or wood putty, applied with a **putty knife**, is used to fill cracks, holes, dents, and nicks so that you will have a smooth, even surface for painting. This can be used on raw wood furniture or even painted and stained furniture. Let dry and sand smooth.

For Priming & Base Painting

Primer:

A primer fills and seals wood and helps paint to bond properly. A **stain blocking primer** keeps old finish from bleeding through new paint. This is especially necessary if you have a dark piece of furniture and want to paint it a light color. Always allow primer to dry thoroughly before base painting.

You can also make your own primer by slightly thinning with water flat white latex wall paint. One coat of this on an old painted or stained piece will help give your surface some "tooth" so that the base paint will adhere properly and smoothly.

Paint for Base Painting:

Base paint is the first layer of paint applied to a surface after the primer. Base paint your furniture piece with **latex wall paint in an eggshell or satin finish, acrylic indoor/outdoor paint**, or **acrylic craft paint**. Brush on the paint, using long, smooth strokes. Work carefully to avoid runs, drips, or sags. All the painting in this book is done with water-based paints. They are easier to use and cleanup and have no odor. Today's new formulas provide just as much wear-and-tear protection as oil-based paints.

Brushes

Base paint can be applied with a **foam brush** or **bristle paint brush**. For painting details or smaller areas, use a 1" **craft brush**. For painting larger flat areas, a **foam roller** is a good choice.

Miscellaneous Supplies

Latex Gloves:

Wear gloves to protect your hands from cleaners, solvents, and paints. These are tight fitting gloves so they will not impair your movements.

Masking Tape:

This is an under-valued supply which I find essential in furniture decorating. Use it to mask off areas for painting, to make crisp lines, and to protect previously painted areas. ⚘

Shown in photo—clockwise beginning at bottom left:
1" craft brush, 2" foam brush, 1-1/2" bristle brush, foam roller, acrylic indoor/outdoor paint, paint thinner, steel wool, latex gloves, paint scraper, paint remover, stain blocking primer, masking tape in a tape dispenser, handheld electric sander, sandpaper, sanding block, putty knife, wood filler, cellulose sponge, soft cloth rag, liquid detergent.

FURNITURE PREPARATION

Photo 1 - Removing hardware.

This section shows how to prepare an old furniture piece by cleaning or stripping and how to prepare new furniture. The purpose of the preparation process is to get a nice flat surface with some tooth to begin your decorating. Study your piece to determine how much preparation needs to be done.

If the finish is in very bad condition or the varnish is wrinkled and chipped, you may choose to strip it. Stripping is usually a last resort, but if you intend to apply a stain or color wash or create a distressed finish that will reveal some of the bare wood, stripping is necessary.

Precautions & Tips

- Read product labels carefully and observe all manufacturer's recommendations and cautions.
- **Always** work in a well-ventilated area or outdoors.
- Wear gloves to protect your hands.
- Wear a dust mask or respirator to protect yourself from dust and fumes.
- Use a piece of old or scrap vinyl flooring for a work surface. Vinyl flooring is more protective and more convenient than layers of newspaper or plastic sheeting. Paint or finishes can seep through newspapers, and newspapers always get stuck to your shoes. Plastic sheeting is slippery. Vinyl flooring is the best solution, and spills can be easily wiped, keeping your working surface dry and clean. Small pieces of vinyl can be purchased inexpensively as remnants from floor covering stores and building supply centers.
- Dispose of solvents properly. If in doubt of how to dispose of them, contact your local government for instructions. Do not pour solvents or paint strippers down drains or toilets.

Photo 2 - Washing a piece with a mild soapy solution.

Choosing a Piece of Furniture

Chances are there's a piece of furniture that's languished for years in your attic, basement, or garage that's a perfect candidate for painting. Tag and yard sales and used furniture stores are other good sources of old furniture. When selecting an old furniture piece, choose one in sound condition. If the legs are wobbly or the drawers stick, make repairs before painting. Repair loose joints with wood glue. If extensive repairs are needed, seek the services of a professional.

Photo 3 - Removing wax buildup with a steel wool pad dipped in paint thinner.

Preparing Old Furniture for Painting

When an old piece of furniture is to receive a painted finish, very often all the piece needs is cleaning and sanding. A primer coat may be necessary if the surface has a glossy varnish. A good rule of thumb is to work with what you see. If your old piece of furniture has a dark finish, perhaps you'll decide to paint it dark green to minimize the amount of preparation you'll need to do, instead of trying to cover up the dark finish with a light paint color.

Step 1 - Remove Hardware:

Before cleaning or sanding, remove all hardware, such as door and drawer pulls. (**photo 1**) Depending upon your piece and what you're planning to do, it also may be necessary to remove hinges, doors, drawers, or mirrors. This is also the time to remove upholstered seats from chairs. Drawer pulls and knobs should be painted or treated while they are detached.

Photo 4 - Sanding a flat surface with sandpaper wrapped around a sanding block.

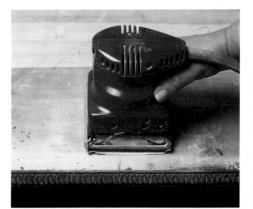

Photo 5 - Sanding a flat surface with a handheld electric finishing sander.

Photo 6 - Sanding in a tight area.

Photo 7 - Filling a crack with wood putty.

Photo 8 - Applying white primer with a bristle paint brush.

Step 2 - Cleaning:

The next step is removing accumulated dust, grease, and grime. Sometimes careful cleaning is all that may be needed before painting. To clean, mix a little mild detergent or bubble bath with water in a bucket or basin. Using a household sponge, wash the piece with the soapy solution. (**photo 2**) Rinse with clear water. Wipe the piece with soft cloth rags to remove surface water. Allow to air dry until the piece is completely dry.

If your piece has years of wax buildup or is covered with shellac or varnish that has cracked or worn unevenly, use a solvent to provide a thorough cleaning and a smooth surface. This is necessary because wax repels waterbased paints, and shellac and varnish are poor undercoats for paint. Pour a solvent such as paint thinner, mineral spirits, or a liquid sandpaper product in a metal can or enamel bowl. Dip a steel wool pad in the solvent and rub the surface (**photo 3**). Rinse the pad in solvent occasionally as you work, and replace the solvent in your container when it gets dirty. When you're finished, allow the piece to air dry.

Step 3 - Sanding:

This is one of the most important steps in the process. Sanding dulls the old finish so new paint will adhere properly and creates a smooth surface for painting. To sand the piece smooth, start with medium grit sandpaper, then use fine grit. Always sand in the direction of the grain. Wrap the sandpaper around a sanding block when sanding on flat surfaces (**photo 4**). Use a hand-held electric finishing sander on larger flat areas, such as tops and shelves (**photo 5**). Hold the sandpaper in your hand when working in tight areas or on curves (**photo 6**). Wipe away dust with a tack cloth. To remove sanding dust from crevices and tight areas, use a brush or a vacuum cleaner.

TIPS:

- When sanding old paint that may contain lead, use wet/dry sandpaper and wet the paper while sanding to prevent creating dust.
- **Always** wear a mask when sanding to prevent inhaling dust.

Step 4 - Filling and Smoothing:

Fill cracks, dents, nicks, and holes with a paste wood filler or wood putty (**photo 7**). Apply the paste with a putty knife, smoothing the material as much as possible and removing any excess before it dries. Follow manufacturer's recommendations regarding drying time. If necessary, apply a second time and let dry thoroughly. Sand smooth when dry. Wipe away dust.

Step 5 - Priming or Undercoating:

Priming or undercoating seals the wood and prevents dark areas from showing through a light colored base paint. Don't use a primer if you intend to apply a stain or color wash. And if you're planning to create a distressed finish that involves sanding through the layers of paint or that will reveal some of the bare wood, don't use primer.

For most finishes, flat white latex wall paint that has been diluted with a little water is an appropriate primer. Mix the paint with a little water (about 10%) to make it go on smoothly.

If your piece has a dark stained or varnished surface, apply a stain blocking white primer so the dark stain or varnish won't bleed through your new paint. Stain blocking primers are also available in brush-on or as sprays (see **photo 8**).

To make your own stain blocking primer, mix equal amounts of white latex wall paint and acrylic varnish. Sponge this mixture over the surface of your piece.

Allow primer to dry overnight. Sand again, lightly, for a smooth surface. Wipe away dust. You're ready to paint!

Step 6 - Base Painting:

Your base paint is your foundation upon which you build your decorative effects. You can sponge over it, rag it, add decorative painted elements, distress it, and antique it. Because it is your foundation, you want it to be smooth and to have thoroughly covered the old paint or finish. Apply the paint with a small roller, or a wide fine-bristled brush. Apply one light coat and allow it to dry. Sand with fine sandpaper to smooth the surface. Apply a second coat and allow to dry thoroughly. If any of the old finish is still showing, apply a third coat. Allow to dry. You are now ready to enjoy your piece or continue with some decorative effects. ◈

Stripping an Old Piece of Furniture

Furniture that was previously painted doesn't need stripping if the finish is sound and not too thick. However, if the existing paint or varnish is chipped, blistered, or cracked, or if the original finish was poorly applied, or if the paint on the piece is so thick it's obscuring the lines or details of the piece, stripping is warranted. You can, of course, have the stripping done by a professional—all you'll need to do is sand the piece afterward. Sometimes it costs less to have a professional do the job than it would to buy the supplies and equipment to do the job yourself.

If you wish to strip the piece yourself, purchase a liquid, gel, or paste product specifically made for the job you're doing. (These generally are labeled "stripper" or "paint remover" and may be waterbased or solvent-based.) Read the label carefully and follow the instructions exactly. Work in a well-ventilated space and wear gloves, goggles, and protective clothing.

Step 1 - Applying the Stripper:

Apply an even layer of stripper to the surface with a bristle brush (**photo 1**) in the direction of the grain of the wood. Work a small portion at a time. Wait the recommended amount of time. The old paint or finish will soften, look wrinkled, and start to lift. Be patient! Chemical strippers give the best results when you allow them enough time to work properly.

Step 2 - Removing the Old Finish:

Use a paint scraper to lift the old finish from the surface (**photo 2**), again working in the direction of the grain. Be careful not to gouge or scrape the surface as you work. On curves, in crevices, and on carved areas, remove the old finish with steel wool, an old brush, toothpicks, or rags.

Step 3 - Sanding:

After the piece has been stripped, it is usually rough. You will need to thoroughly sand your piece. See section, "Preparing Old Furniture for Painting" for tips on sanding. After a thorough sanding with medium, then fine sandpaper, you are now ready for basepainting or staining. ❧

Photo 1 - *Applying the stripper with a bristle brush.*

Photo 2 - *Lifting the softened old finish with a paint scraper.*

Preparing New Unfinished Wood Furniture

New unfinished wood furniture requires less preparation than old furniture—often sanding and priming are all that's necessary.

Step 1 - Sanding:

Sand the furniture with fine grit sandpaper, sanding with the grain of the wood, to remove rough edges and smooth the surface. Use a sanding block (**photo 3**) or handheld electric sander on flat surfaces. Hold the paper in your hand on curved areas. Remove dust with a tack cloth or a dry dust cloth. Don't use a damp cloth—the dampness could raise the grain of the wood.

On some furniture, glue may have seeped out of the joints. It's important to remove any glue residue—paint won't adhere to it. If possible, sand away the dried glue. If sanding doesn't remove it, scrape it lightly with a craft knife.

Photo 3 - *Sanding with a sanding block.*

Photo 4 - *Sealing with shellac.*

Photo 5 - *Applying a primer.*

Step 2 - Sealing (Optional):

If there are knots or dark places on the piece, seal them with clear sealer or shellac (**photo 4**). Let dry completely. This will keep any sap or residue from bleeding through the base paint coat.

Step 3 - Filling (Optional):

If your piece has nail holes, gaps, or cracks, fill them with wood filler or wood putty, using a putty knife. Smooth the material as much as possible and remove any excess before it dries. Follow manufacturer's recommendations regarding drying time. When dry, sand smooth. Wipe away dust.

Step 4 - Priming:

Do this step only if you are going to cover the piece with an opaque coat of base paint. If you plan on staining, pickling, or color washing your piece, then you will not need to do this step.

Paint the piece with a coat of diluted flat white latex wall paint (mixed by adding about 10% water to paint) or use a commercial primer (**photo 5**). Let dry thoroughly. Sand with fine sandpaper. Wipe away dust with a tack cloth.

Step 5 - Base Painting:

Your base paint is your foundation upon which you build your decorative effects. You can sponge over it, rag it, add decorative painted elements, distress it, and antique it. Because it is your foundation, you want it to be smooth and to have thoroughly covered the wood underneath. Apply the paint with a small roller, or a wide fine-bristled brush. Apply one light coat and allow it to dry. Sand with fine sandpaper to smooth the surface. Apply a second coat and allow to dry thoroughly. If any of the the old finish is still showing, apply a third coat. Allow to dry. You are now ready to enjoy your piece or continue with some decorative effects. ❧

Finishing Your Project

If you haven't used an indoor/outdoor paint for your decorating, then you will want to give your finished piece a protective coating. Varnishes and sealers are available in a variety of finishes—matte, satin, and gloss. Satin is my favorite—it gives a nice lustre yet does not emphasize any uneven brush strokes. A glossy finish allows any unevenness to show.

Use waterbase varnishes and sealers that are compatible with acrylic paints for sealing and finishing. They are available in brush on and spray formulations. Choose products that are non-yellowing and quick drying.

Apply the finish according to the manufacturer's instructions. Several thin coats are better than one thick coat (**photo 6**). Let dry between coats according to the manufacturer's recommendations. A furniture piece such as a breakfast table, which will receive a lot of use, will need more coats of sealer or varnish for protection. ❧

Photo 6: *Applying waterbase varnish with a foam brush*

SUPPLIES

for decorating furniture

Paint

Because waterbase paints have so many advantages and are so readily available, the paint recommendations in this book have been limited to waterbase paints. Some advantages include:

- They have less odor because they contain far less solvent than oil-base paints, and so are much less apt to provoke headache or nausea. Some types are considered non-toxic.
- Cleanup is easy with soap and water, so the painter is not exposed to solvents in the cleaning of tools or brushes.
- They are safer to use indoors and not nearly as polluting as solvent based paints in their manufacturing process or in the volatile organic compounds (VOCs) they release after application.

Types of Paint for Base Painting, Color Block Painting, and Decorative Painting

- **Latex wall paint** is a good choice for base painting a larger furniture piece. It can be custom mixed to virtually any color and is available in quart and gallon quantities. Use flat white for a primer coat. Use an eggshell or satin finish for base painting your piece. You can buy latex wall paint at paint stores, hardware stores, and building supply centers.
- **Acrylic craft paints** are ideal for base painting smaller pieces, for adding painting accents or painting small areas, and for decorative painting. They also can be used for stenciling and stamping. Acrylic craft paints are available in a huge range of colors, are highly pigmented, and of excellent quality. These are most often sold in 2 oz. plastic squeeze bottles. They can be found in craft shops in the decorative painting section.
- **Acrylic artist's paints** are highly pigmented acrylic paints that are available in traditional artist's pigment colors. They are used for decorative painting. These are most often found in tubes or in 2 oz. plastic squeeze bottles. They can be found in craft shops in the decorative painting section.
- **Acrylic painting mediums** are used with acrylic craft paints or artist's paints in decorative painting to help accomplish a particular effect, such as blending, floating, or extending drying time. They can be found in craft shops in the decorative painting section and at art supply stores.
- **Acrylic indoor/outdoor paints** are suitable for indoor and outdoor use and generally come in 8 oz. jars. This size is usually enough paint for a small or medium size piece, such as a chair or small table. The color range is not as wide as that of acrylic craft paints. Indoor/outdoor paints don't require varnishing. They can be found in home decorating stores or crafts stores.
- **Stencil Paints:** Stenciling can be successfully accomplished with acrylic craft paints. In addition to acrylic craft paints, other types of paint are made just for stenciling. **Stencil gels** have a subtle transparency and a thick gel formula. **Cream stencil paints**, which come in small jars, and **stick paints**, which look like big crayons, also can be used to stencil on furniture. They are found in home decorating and crafts stores.
- **Neutral Glazing Medium** is a colorless, full-bodied liquid or gel that can be tinted with colored paint glaze, latex paint, or acrylic craft paint. It is used to create sponged, stippled, brushed, and other textured effects and to add a transparent colored glaze over painted surfaces. Mix paint or glaze in disposable receptacles such as plastic buckets, foam bowl, or plastic cups.

Brushes for Applying Paint

Base paint with a **foam brush** or **bristle paint brush**. Use a 1" **craft brush** for smaller areas. A **foam roller** can make quick work of a large, flat area.

For decorative design painting, use **artist's paint brushes**. Flats are used for applying color and blending, rounds are used for applying color and painting shapes, and liners are used for details.

All types of stencil paint can be applied with **stencil brushes** using a swirling or pouncing motion. Stencil brushes, which are round and have short bristles, also can be used for some decorative painting techniques. A small **foam roller** also can be used for stenciling.

Other Supplies & Tools for Decorating

- **Pre-cut stencils** are quick and easy ways to add design motifs and lettering to painted furniture. You can also cut your own stencils from stencil blank material with a **craft knife** or cut sponges from dense foam material with scissors or a craft knife. Most craft departments or home centers have a wide variety of stencils from which to choose. Even stencils labled for wall decorating can be used on furniture.
- **Stamps** are now available in large design motifs that are perfect for furniture decorating. These types of stamps are made of foam and are flexible (not to be confused with rubber stamps). Paint is applied to the design and then it is stamped on the surface.
- **Tools for creating textured finishes** include the **French brush** and **stippler brush** for stippled or brushed textures. **Sea sponges, cellulose sponges**, and **sponging mitts** are used for sponging. A **spatter tool** (a screen with a special brush) or an old toothbrush or bristle brush can be used for spattering or flyspecking to add random dots of color. Combing tool for creating textured lines.
- **Masking tape** can be used to mask off borders and stripes. Choose a tape that's labeled "low tack." Low tack tape won't leave a residue, and it is easy to remove. ❧

Shown in photo clockwise, beginning at bottom left: *craft knife, masking tape, pre-cut stencil, stencil brush, combing tool, spatter tool, French brush, stippler brush, pencil, indoor/outdoor acrylic paint, neutral glazing medium, foam bowl for mixing, sponging mitt, cellulose sponge, natural sea sponge, pre-cut foam stamps, acrylic craft paint, foam brush, four artist's paint brushes (**from top,** liner, round, two flats), 1-1/2" bristle basecoat brush.*

THE PROJECTS

The projects in this book were carefully chosen to present an array of painting techniques and decorative styles. Many projects are easy to do and can be accomplished in an afternoon or a weekend. The projects range in complexity from simple pieces perfect for beginners that employ color block painting, stamping, stenciling, to more advanced projects that include decorative painting and faux finishing techniques. There are step-by-step instructions and numerous photographs to guide you.

Try your hand at stenciling the Fish Stories Bookcase, and use what you learned to stencil your chosen design on a chest, armoire, or chair. Use the motif from the Magnolia Armoire to create a coordinating headboard. Paint a special chair for a special friend in her favorite colors. Create fun furniture for children's rooms. Use the ideas presented with each project as a springboard for designing and personalizing your own furniture. Have fun being your own furniture designer!

FISH STORIES

stenciled bookcase

Vibrant colors combined with stencils and stamps tell a tropical tale on this ordinary bookcase. Aquatic motifs are stenciled and stamped within postcard size blocks of bright color and framed with checked borders. Inside the bookshelf, the same motifs are arranged for the look of an aquarium.

Created by Kathi Malarchuk

1
Supplies

Furniture Piece:
Wooden bookcase

Acrylic craft paint:
for stenciling and stamping
    Black
    Light blue
    Chartreuse
    Bright yellow
    Fuchsia
    Golden yellow
    Peach, 4 oz.
    Purple
    Teal
    White

Latex wall paint, eggshell finish
for base painting the bookcase
    1 qt. turquoise
    1 qt. lime green
    1 qt. light yellow

Tools & Other Supplies:
Pre-cut stencil - fish (contains 3 fish, 8",
    5 1/2", and 4")
Pre-cut stamps - starfish 4" dia., and nautilus
    shell, 3 1/2"
Masking tape
Stencil brushes
Sponge brushes OR small foam paint roller
Palette OR palette paper
Artist's paint brushes, #2 flat
Pencil with new eraser
Brown paper bags
Waterbase varnish

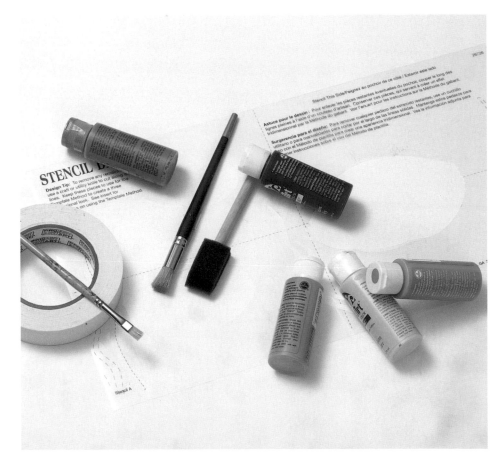

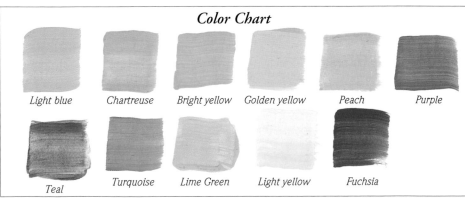

Color Chart

Light blue	Chartreuse	Bright yellow	Golden yellow	Peach	Purple
Teal	Turquoise	Lime Green	Light yellow	Fuchsia	

Instructions follow on page 20

2
Preparation

Prepare the bookcase for painting, following the instructions in the "Furniture Preparation" section.

3
Base Painting

Use photo as a guide for color placement.

1. Base paint sides of bookcase with turquoise wall paint.
2. Base paint inside back and sides with lime green wall paint.
3. Base paint top flat surface with peach acrylic craft paint. Let dry completely.
4. Base paint shelves with light yellow wall paint.
5. Base paint front rims of shelves and rim around top with chartreuse acrylic craft paint.

4
Painting the Backgrounds

1. Measure fish on fish stencil. Add 2" to each dimension to determine sizes of background rectangles.
2. Mask off rectangles on both sides of bookcase, overlapping as shown in photo. Paint backgrounds with acrylic craft paint colors — (from the top down) — chartreuse, light blue, peach, bright yellow, golden yellow, purple (**photo 1**). Let dry. Remove tape.

5
Stamping & Stenciling

1. Stencil fish and seaweed with acrylic craft paints inside some of the frames, using photo as a guide for placement and colors (**photo 2**). Seaweed is teal. Use fuchsia and purple for the large fish stencil on the chartreuse block. Stencil fuchsia lightly for body and more solid for fins. Use golden yellow, fuchsia and purple for the large fish on the purple block. Use teal, golden yellow and fuchsia for the medium fish. Use purple and light blue for small fish.
2. Stencil more fish and seaweed inside the bookcase.
3. Apply peach acrylic craft paint to starfish stamp with a sponge brush. Stamp inside the bookcase. See photo for placement.
4. Apply purple acrylic craft paint to starfish stamp and stamp inside one of the frames.
5. Apply fuchsia acrylic craft paint to shell stamp with a sponge brush. Stamp inside frames and inside the bookcase. See photo for placement.

Continued on next page

Photo 1. *Mask off rectangles with tape and paint with various colors. Use a small paint roller or a sponge brush.*

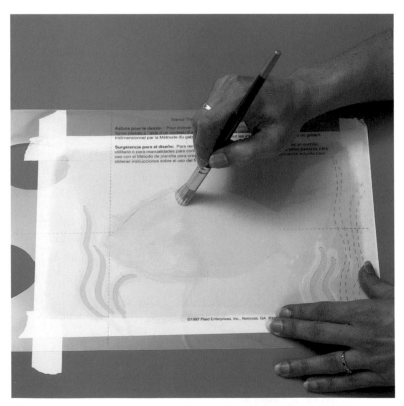

Photo 2. *Position fish stencil so the fish is centered inside the frame. Stencil fish with acrylic craft paint, using a stencil brush and very little paint. Concentrate the color on the edges of the stencil.*

Continued from page 20

6
Painting the Frames & Borders

1. Mask off a frame 1/4" wide around each painted rectangle. Mask off borders 1/4" wide on the top and bottom edges of front rims of shelves. Paint frames and borders white. Let dry.
2. Using a #2 flat brush, paint checks on frames and borders with black (**photo 3**). Let dry. Remove tape.
3. Using a pencil eraser or the handle end of the #2 flat brush, stamp random dots on the front rims of the shelves between the checked borders with teal paint. Simply dip the eraser or the end of the brush in paint and press on the surface. Use the same technique to make air bubbles from the mouths of the fish inside the bookcase. Let dry completely.

7
Finishing

Apply two to three coats waterbase varnish. Let dry between coats and buff with pieces of a brown paper bag. ঌ

Photo 3. *Use single strokes of black paint to create the checks on the frames. The width of the check is the width of the #2 flat brush.*

Closeup of bookcase side

BRIGHT AS A MELON

painted 60s chair

Four paint colors and a simple design transform an outdated dining room chair from the 1960s into something special. A set of them could brighten up the eating area of a kitchen or a covered porch—or just use one as an accent in any room that needs touches of whimsy and color.

Created by Jeff McWilliams

1
Supplies

Furniture Piece:
Wooden chair with spindle back

Acrylic Craft Paint:
Black
Green
Red
White

Tools & Other Supplies:
1/2" paint brush
1" paint brush
Sandpaper, medium grit
Tracing paper
Transfer paper & stylus
Gloss sealer spray

2
Preparation

Prepare the chair for painting, following the instructions in the "Furniture Preparation" section.

3
Base Painting

Use photo as a guide for color placement.
1. Paint the legs and bottom of the seat green. Use as many coats as needed to achieve opaque coverage. Let dry and sand lightly between coats.
2. Paint top of the seat and back spindles red. Use as many coats as needed to achieve opaque coverage. Let dry and sand lightly between coats.
3. Paint the top rail of the back black. Use as many coats as needed to achieve opaque coverage. Let dry and sand lightly between coats.

4
Design Painting

1. Trace the watermelon seed pattern and transfer to the seat, using photo as a guide for placement.
2. Paint the seeds black.
3. Using the 1/2" paint brush, lightly pounce white paint around the edge of top of the seat.
4. Add a faint white highlight to the left side of each seed. Let dry completely.

5
Finishing

Spray with two coats gloss sealer. Let dry between coats. ❧

Pattern for Watermelon Seed

TWO PAIRS OF PEARS
dimensional ornamented table

Two pairs of painted wooden pears adorn the corners of this fanciful table. The purchased pre-cut wood pieces add dimension and ornamentation; bright blocks of color keep the design simple and crisp.

Created by Jeff McWilliams

1
Supplies

Furniture Piece:
Rectangular wooden table with curved apron and tall, thin legs

Wood Trim Pieces:
4 wooden pears, 2" high
4 wooden carrots, 1-1/2" long, 3/16" thick (they are used for the pears' leaves and stems)
24 wooden dolls' heads, 3/4" diameter (dolls' heads are round but one side is flattened)

Acrylic Craft Paint:
Bright yellow
Kelly green
Deep blue
Light brown
Medium yellow
Purple
Teal

Tools & Other Supplies:
Stippling brush OR 1" stencil brush
1" paint brush
Wood glue
Matte sealer spray
Sandpaper, medium grit
Optional: masking tape

2
Preparation

Prepare the table for painting, following the instructions in the "Furniture Preparation" section.

3
Painting the Table

Use photo as a guide for color placement.
1. Paint the table apron with two coats medium yellow. Let dry and sand lightly between coats.
2. Using stippling brush or stencil brush, pounce bright yellow over the medium yellow base paint. Let some of the base paint show through the stippling. Let dry overnight.
3. Mask off the top of the apron to protect it. Paint the table top with two coats purple. Let dry and sand between coats. When second coat is dry, remove tape.
4. Paint the legs with two coats teal. Let dry and sand between coats.

4
Painting the Wood Trim Pieces

Use photo as a guide for color placement. All pieces require two coats. Let dry between coats.
1. Paint the pears bright yellow.
2. The carrots will be the stems and leaves of the pears. Paint the stem areas light brown. Paint the leaf areas Kelly green.
3. Paint the doll heads deep blue.

5
Assembling and Finishing

1. Glue the painted carrots (which are now the leaves and stems) to the tops of the pears. See photo.
2. Glue the painted doll heads to the table apron. Use photo as a guide for placement. There are five on each end and seven on each side.
3. Glue a pear at each corner of the table.
4. Spray the entire table with matte sealer. ✍

Pictured left: Dimensional wooden pieces were painted and glued to decorate the table.

DIAMONDS & GOLD

stenciled & distressed chest

Lightly sanded layers of color create a soft, aged finish on this chest of drawers. The wide stripes on the front were masked off with tape. A stencil was used for the diamond shapes on the sides and top, and golden circles between the diamonds were stamped with a round sponge applicator.

Created by Kathi Malarchuk

1
Supplies

Furniture Piece:
Wooden chest of drawers

Latex wall paint:
Off white
Golden tan

Other Paint:
Glazing medium - neutral
Colored paint glaze - brown
Acrylic craft paint - gold metallic

Tools & Other Supplies:
5/8" round sponge applicator (for stamping circles)
Diamond stencil OR stencil blank material, permanent marker, and craft knife
Sea sponge
Sandpaper, fine grit, and sanding block OR electric finishing sander
Measuring tape
Chalk pencil
Masking tape
Sponge brushes
Palette OR palette paper
Drawer pulls

Photo 1: *Wrap a piece of sandpaper around a sanding block and sand the painted surface to create a worn, distressed look. An electric finishing sander could also be used, but work carefully so you don't remove the base paint.*

2
Preparation & Base Painting

1. Remove drawer pulls. Prepare the chest for painting, following the instructions in the "Furniture Preparation" section.
2. Paint with two coats of white latex paint. Let dry and sand between coats. Let second coat dry completely.

3
Painting the Stripes

1. Measure and mask off stripes 4" wide on drawer fronts and front of chest. Paint with golden tan latex paint. Let dry. Keep tape in place.
2. Mix 1 part brown colored glaze with 2 parts neutral glazing medium. Sponge tan stripes with glaze mixture. Let dry. Remove tape. Reserve remaining glaze mixture.

4
Stenciling the Diamonds

1. Using photo as a guide, determine how you wish to place the diamond shapes on the sides and top of the chest. You may wish to draw some guidelines with a pencil to keep diamonds straight. *If you're not using a pre-cut stencil,* draw a diamond shape on stencil blank material and cut out with a craft knife.
2. Position the stencil on the top and sides of the chest and stencil the diamonds with golden tan latex paint. Let dry.
3. Sponge diamonds with the reserved glaze mixture with stencil in place. Let dry.

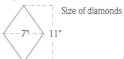
Size of diamonds
7"   11"

5
Stamping the Circles

Load the 5/8" round sponge applicator with gold metallic paint. Stamp gold circles at points where diamonds meet. See photo for placement. Load stamp for each pressing so the look will be uniform. Let dry completely.

6
Distressing

Sand over painted stripes, diamonds, and circles on drawer fronts, top, front, and sides of chest to remove some of the layers of paint and expose the white base paint (**photo 1**). Remove more paint on areas that would be naturally worn, such as edges and corners. Wipe away sanding dust.

7
Finishing

1. Seal chest with two to three coats waterbase varnish, following manufacturer's instructions. Let dry.
2. Install drawer pulls. ⑤

FLOWER POWER

bar stool with handpainted daisies

With just a little paint and time, an ordinary bar stool can be the best seat in the house! Sponge shapes are used to stamp the raspberry flower centers and random white squares, and the yellow daisy petals are simple to paint. The spiral-striped legs are easy to create with tape.

Created by Kathi Malarchuk

1
Supplies

Furniture Piece:
Wooden bar stool

Indoor/Outdoor Paint:
Sage green
Off white
Teal green

Acrylic Craft Paint:
Use gloss acrylic enamel paints.
Raspberry
White
Yellow

Tools & Other Supplies:
1-3/4" round sponge applicator (for stamping circles)
Sponge square, 2"
Masking tape
Artist's paint brush - #5 round
Tracing paper
Transfer paper and stylus

2
Preparation & Base Painting

1. Prepare the stool for painting, following the instructions in the "Furniture Preparation" section.
2. Paint seat and cross rungs with sage green. Let dry completely.
3. Paint legs with off white. Let dry completely.
4. Using photo as a guide, wrap masking tape around each leg to create a spiral stripe (like a barber pole). Paint legs with teal green. Let dry. Remove tape.

3
Design Painting

1. Use 2" sponge square to randomly stamp squares on top with white. Use photo as a guide for placement. Let dry.
2. Trace patterns for daisy petals and transfer randomly to top and rungs of stool. Paint petals with yellow, using a #5 round brush. Let dry.
3. Use the round sponge applicator to stamp daisy centers with raspberry.

See page 30 for project patterns.

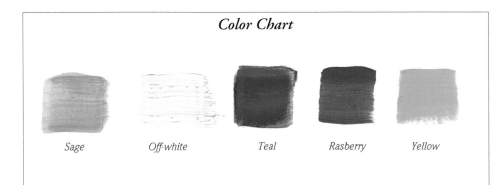

Color Chart

| Sage | Off-white | Teal | Rasberry | Yellow |

Patterns for Daisies

Use small daisy for rungs of stool.

Closeup of stool top

BUSY BEES

stippled & stenciled cupboard

The bees can't help but be attracted to this honey-colored cupboard with a honeycomb motif stenciled on the door. Use it in a kitchen or breakfast room to display a special treat or to add sweetness and light to any room in the house.

Created by Jeff McWilliams

1
Supplies

Furniture Piece:
Wooden cupboard with hinged door

Wood Trim Pieces:
18 half eggs, 2" long, 1-3/8" wide
36 teardrop shapes (triangles with two
  rounded corners), 1" long

Latex Wall Paint, Eggshell Finish:
  Golden yellow

Acrylic Craft Paint:
  Black
  Bright yellow
  Burnt orange
  Deep blue
  Golden tan
  Mustard
  White

Tools & Other Supplies:
1" stencil brush
Stippling brush
1" paint brush
Sandpaper, medium grit
Matte sealer spray
Masking tape, 3/4"
Wood glue
Brown antiquing medium
Honeycomb pattern stencil OR stencil
  blank material, black permanent marker,
  and craft knife

2
Preparation & Base Painting

1. Remove door, hinges, and door pull.
2. Prepare the cupboard for painting, following the instructions in the "Furniture Preparation" section.
3. Paint the cupboard—sides, door, top, inside—with two coats golden yellow latex wall paint. Let dry and sand between coats.
4. Paint the top with one coat burnt orange. Let dry completely.
5. Sand the top, removing some of the paint, for a worn look. Wipe away dust.

continued on page 34

Dimensional wooden pieces to paint and glue for bee decoration.

continued from page 32

3
Stippling and Stenciling

1. Using the stippling brush, pounce the sides of the cabinet—but not the door or the top—with golden tan (**photo 1**).
2. *If you don't have a honeycomb pattern stencil,* trace the pattern below on stencil blank material, using a permanent marker. Cut out stencil with a craft knife.
3. Stencil honeycomb design on inside of door panel with mustard.

4
Taping Off & Painting Stripes

1. Using photo as a guide, tape off stripes 3/4" wide on door frame with 3/4" masking tape.
2. Paint stripes with burnt orange (**photo 2**). Let dry. Remove tape (**photo 3**).

5
Making the Bees

1. Paint the half eggs (they will be the bees' bodies) bright yellow.
2. Paint the teardrops (they will be the bees' wings) white.
3. Paint three horizontal stripes on each bee's body with black.
4. Glue two wings to each bee's body. Use photo as a guide.

Photo 1. *Using the stippling brush, pounce the sides of the cabinet with golden tan.*

Photo 2. *Mask off stripes on door frame with tape. Paint with burnt orange.*

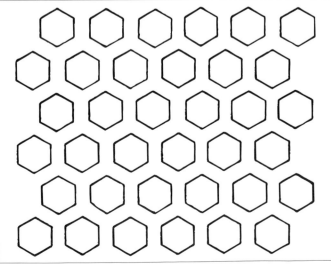
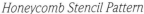

Honeycomb Stencil Pattern

Photo 3. *Remove tape to reveal striped border on door frame.*

6
Antiquing, Assembling & Finishing

1. Apply antiquing medium to all surfaces of the cabinet—top, sides, and door—and to the bees. Let dry.
2. Paint the door pull deep blue. Let dry.
3. Attach door and hinges to cabinet. Attach door pull.
4. Attach bees to cabinet with wood glue, using photo as a guide for placement.
5. Spray all surfaces with matte sealer. ❧

Closeup of cabinet

POSIES, STRIPES & SWIRLS

handpainted corrugated child's rocking chair

A child's rocking chair, assembled from pre-cut corrugated cardboard, becomes a flower garden of delight with simple painting techniques. What a wonderful welcome for a visiting grandchild!

Created by Allison Stilwell

1
Supplies

Furniture Piece:
Child's corrugated cardboard rocking chair

Latex Wall Paint:
Ecru

Acrylic Craft Paint:
   Black
   Kelly green
   Fuchsia
   Yellow
   Purple
   Chartreuse

Artist's Paint Brushes:
Flats - #6, #8
Script liner - #1

Tools & Other Supplies:
Glazing medium - neutral (a 2 oz. bottle is
   enough)
Masking tape, 2" wide
Round sponge applicators - 3/4", 1-3/4"
Sponge brushes
Matte acrylic sealer spray

Color Chart

Kelly Green   Fuchsia   Yellow

Purple   Chartreuse

2
Base Painting

Base paint the entire chair—all the pieces—with ecru. Let dry.

3
Design Painting

Back:
See "How to Paint Posies, Leaves & Vines" page 38.
1. Paint purple on both sides. Let dry.
2. To make posies, paint random rounded shapes with yellow.
3. Using a #6 flat brush, paint leaves with kelly green. Let dry.
4. Add black outlines and details to flowers and leaves, using a #1 script liner.

Leg Braces:
1. Paint both sides purple. Let dry.
2. On front side of each piece, paint kelly green stripes 1/2" wide. *TIP: A #8 flat brush loaded with paint will make a stripe 1/2" wide.*

Seat:
1. Mask off stripes 2" wide on seat with tape. Mix equal amounts glazing medium and yellow paint.
2. Paint unmasked stripes with yellow glaze mixture. Remove tape. Let dry.

Sides:
1. Paint the insides of the side pieces chartreuse. Let dry.
2. Mix equal amounts glazing medium and kelly green to make a transparent green. Paint the outsides of the side pieces with the green glaze mixture. Let dry.
3. To make a flower, stamp four purple circles using the 1-3/4" sponge applicator. Let dry. Stamp the flower centers with yellow, using the 3/4" sponge applicator. Stamp the flowers randomly on the outsides of the side pieces. Use photo as a guide for placement.
4. Add spirals with fuchsia, using a #1 script liner. Let dry.

4
Finishing

1. Spray both sides of all pieces with matte sealer. Let dry completely.
2. Assemble chair according to manufacturer's instructions. ❧

See page 39 for project patterns

How to Paint Posies, Leaves & Vines
Painting Worksheet

Posies and leaves are easy to paint freehand. Here are some examples:

Fig. 1 - Posies:

1. Paint random rounded shapes with the color or colors you want your flowers to be. (Shown here are lavender flower shapes and pale yellow flower shapes accented with pink.) Let dry.
2. Add green leaves. See Fig. 2 and 3. Let dry.
3. Using a script liner with black paint, add a swirly outline around the flower shape. Add a few lines inside the shape to suggest petals and a center. Outline the leaves. For smaller posies, you can use a fine tip black permanent marker to add the details.

Fig. 2 - Flat Brush Leaves:

Load the brush with paint. Place it on the surface where you want the leaf to be. Pull the brush and, as you pull, turn the brush 90 degrees to make the pointed end of the leaf. The size of the leaf depends on the size of the brush you use, but the technique is the same.

Fig. 3 - Round Brush Leaves:

Load the brush with paint. Place the brush where you want the leaf to be. Pull away and up.

Fig. 4 - Vines:

1. Using a liner brush, paint wavy green lines.
2. With the liner brush or a small round brush, add lots of leaves.

Fig. 5 - Dot Flowers:

Dot flowers are formed by four dots of one color and a dot in the center that's another color. Make them in different colors and sizes and you can have a bouquet or a garden.

Posies, Stripes, & Swirls - Rocking Chair: pictured on page 37.

Pattern for Lamp Sides &
Back of Chair

Chair Sides

Posies Go Round - Lamp: pictured on page 47.
Pattern for Top

*Hearts & Flowers - Footstool:
pictured on page 43*

Pattern - Top of Stool

Posies - Shelf:
pictured on page 44, 45

Refer to photo for placement of patterns.

HEARTS & FLOWERS

handpainted footstool

This charming little footstool would make a happy addition to any room. Use it in a child's room bathroom so the sink can be reached, or beside a bed to hold all those stacks of magazines, or in a kitchen so that the top shelf is within reach. There are so many possibilities for something this pretty.
Pale pink hearts are nestled among the posies that top a footstool painted in pretty pastels. On this stool, the legs are divided into three parts by the bevels in the turnings. If your stool has straight legs, divide the legs into three sections and tape off for painting, using the photo as a guide. Separate the sections with narrow bands of color.

Created by Allison Stilwell

1
Supplies

Furniture Piece:
Wooden footstool

Acrylic Craft Paint:
Cream
Deep purple
Green
Lavender
Pale pink
Golden yellow
Pale yellow
Pale lavender
Red violet
Yellow

Latex wall paint, eggshell finish:
Chartreuse, 1 pint is enough

Artist's Paint Brushes:
Shader - #4
Script liner - #1
Basecoater - #8

Tools & Other Supplies:
1" foam brush
Tracing paper
Transfer paper & stylus
Waterbase varnish
Optional: masking tape

2
Preparation & Base Painting

1. Prepare the stool for painting, following the instructions in the "Furniture Preparation" section.
2. Base paint the stool with chartreuse latex paint. Let dry.

3
Design Painting

Legs:
1. Decorate the lower section of each leg with tiny dot flowers. The petals are dots of red violet. The centers are dots of yellow. The leaves are green. See "How to Paint Posies, Leaves & Vines."
2. Paint the rounded bevels cream. Let dry.
3. Add vertical stripes to the rounded bevels with golden yellow, using a #4 shader. See photo for spacing.

Top:
1. Paint the top of the stool pale lavender. Paint the edges cream.
2. Dilute a small amount of green with water to make a wash. Using a 1" foam brush, add vertical stripes around the edges of the top with this wash. Let dry.
3. Trace and transfer the pattern for the stool.
4. Paint the flower petals pale yellow. As you paint, add touches of yellow to your brush now and then.
5. Paint hearts pale pink.
6. Paint leaves green.
7. Paint flower centers lavender. Let dry.
8. Add dots of yellow to flower centers. Let dry.
9. Using a #1 script liner with deep purple, outline and add details to the leaves, flowers, and hearts. Let dry.

4
Finishing

Apply several coats waterbase varnish. Let dry between coats. ❧

See page 40 for project patterns.

POSIES

shelf

Fanciful flowers adorn the sides and back of this colorful wall shelf. This shelf will add a charming touch to breakfast nook, child's room, bathroom, or bedroom. The flowers are easy and fun to paint freehand. You can also use the pattern provided to transfer to the shelf. For a detailed look at how to paint them, see the Painting Worksheet, "How to Paint Posies, Leaves & Vines."

Created by Allison Stilwell

1
Supplies

Furniture Piece:
Wooden wall shelf, 18 3/4" wide

Acrylic Craft Paint:

Golden yellow	Green
Hot pink	Lilac
Pale pink	Chartreuse
Aqua	Pale lavender, 4 oz.
Plum	

Artist's Paint Brushes:
Shader - #12
Script liner - #1
Flat - #12

Tools & Other Supplies:
1" foam brush
Waterbase varnish

See page 41 for project patterns

Color Chart

Golden yellow	*Green*	*Hot Pink*
Lilac	*Pale pink*	*Chartreuse*
Aqua	*Plum*	*Pale Lavender*

2
Preparation & Base Painting

All base painting and design painting is done with acrylic craft paint, which is most often sold in 2 oz. bottles.

1. Prepare the shelf for painting and prime, following the instructions in the "Furniture Preparation" section.
2. Base paint the back of the shelf with pale lavender. Let dry.
3. Paint shelf and ends with chartreuse.
4. Paint front edges with golden yellow. Let dry.
5. Paint the inner sides with pale pink.

3
Design Painting

Back of Shelf:
See "How to Paint Posies, Leaves & Vines."

1. Paint posies on the back of the shelf. First, paint random rounded shapes with plum. Let dry. Paint slightly smaller shapes on top of the plum shapes with lilac, leaving the plum showing on the edges. Let dry.
2. Using a script liner with pale lavender paint, add swirly lines inside the flower shapes to suggest petals and a center.
3. Add green leaves. Let dry.
4. Paint veins on the leaves with chartreuse. Let dry.

Edges:

1. Paint a wavy line across the front edge with aqua.

2. Add dots of hot pink. Let dry.

3. Add small dots of lilac inside the hot pink dots.

4. On the side edges, use a #12 shader with green to create horizontal stripes the width of the brush. Let dry.

Inner Sides:

1. Using a ruler and pencil, measure and lightly mark diagonal lines 1-1/2" apart to form a lattice design on the inner sides.

2. Paint lattice with green.

3. Paint flowers, using curved strokes to make small rounded shapes inside each section of the lattice with hot pink. (Leaving some space between your strokes makes them look like roses.) Let dry.

4. Add two small leaves to each flower with green.

Outer Sides:

1. Mix equal amounts green and aqua. Paint wavy vines along curved edges on sides. Add leaves on the vines. Let dry.

2. Add tiny dot flowers to the vines. Paint petals with plum. Add centers with golden yellow. Let dry.

4
Finishing

Apply two to three coats waterbase varnish. Let dry between coats. ❧

POSIES GO ROUND

bedside lamp

Painted with cheerful colors and adorned with stripes, flowers, dots and swirls, this lamp is sure to brighten any corner. For a detailed look at how to paint the flowers, see the Painting Worksheet, "How to Paint Posies, Leaves & Vines."

Created by Allison Stilwell

1
Supplies

Furniture Piece:
Lamp with square wooden base

Acrylic Craft Paint:

Black   Yellow   Green
Aqua   Pale pink   Pale yellow
Peach   Violet   Warm white
Golden yellow

Artist's Paint Brushes:
Script liner - #1
Small round brush
Flat - #12

Tools & Other Supplies:
1" foam brush
Tracing paper
Transfer paper & stylus
Cellophane tape OR masking tape, 1/2" wide
Primer
Waterbase varnish

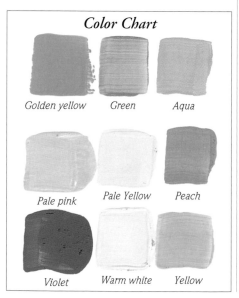

Color Chart

Golden yellow   Green   Aqua

Pale pink   Pale Yellow   Peach

Violet   Warm white   Yellow

2
Preparation & Base Painting

All base painting and design painting is done with acrylic craft paint, which is most often sold in 2 oz. bottles.

1. Prepare lamp base for painting and prime, following the instructions in the "Furniture Preparation" section.
2. Paint the feet, bottom edge trim, and two opposite sides with yellow. Let dry.
3. Paint the top edge trim with pale yellow. Let dry.
4. On the same two opposite sides, tape off stripes 1/2" apart. Paint stripes with aqua. Let dry. Apply a second coat. Let dry. Remove tape.
5. Paint two other sides with pale pink. Let dry.
6. Paint the top violet. Let dry.
7. Trace pattern for lamp. Transfer to top of lamp base.

3
Design Painting

Sides:
See "How to Paint Posies, Leaves & Vines."

1. Paint posies on the striped sides, using photo as a guide for placement. First, paint random rounded shapes with warm white and golden yellow. As you paint the petals, add touches of yellow and peach to your brush. Let dry.
2. Add green leaves. Let dry.
3. Using a script liner with black paint, add swirly lines inside the flower shapes to suggest petals and a center. Outline leaves and paint center veins.
4. On the pink sides, use a script liner to paint swirls of golden yellow. Use photo as a guide.

Feet:
Using a small round brush, add aqua dots to feet.

Top:
1. Paint posies with the same colors used on the sides of the lamp.
2. Outline and add details to posies and leaves with black, using a #1 script liner.
3. Paint the lettering ("Ring around the Rosies") with black, using a #1 script liner. Let dry.

4
Finishing

Apply two coats waterbase varnish. Let dry between coats. ❧

See page 39 for project patterns.

DON'T BUG ME

handpainted step stool

Bugs—both realistic and whimsical—decorate this colorful step stool with a message. Patterns are provided for the bugs, but don't be afraid to make up your own designs. The world is full of wild and wonderful creatures, so you can't really go wrong.

Created by Allison Stilwell

1
Supplies

Furniture Piece:
Wooden step stool

Latex wall paint, eggshell finish:
White, 8 oz. is enough

Acrylic Craft Paints:

Aqua	Black	Blue (metallic)
Fuchsia	Orange	Chartreuse
Pale pink	Purple	Yellow

Artist's Paint Brushes:
Shader - #12
Script liner - #1

Tools & Other Supplies:
Tracing paper
Transfer paper & stylus
1" sponge brush
Waterbase varnish

See pages 51 - 53 for project patterns.

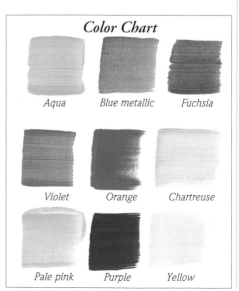

Color Chart

Aqua	Blue metallic	Fuchsia
Violet	Orange	Chartreuse
Pale pink	Purple	Yellow

2
Preparation & Base Painting

1. Prepare step stool for painting, following the instructions in the "Furniture Preparation" section.
2. Base paint the stool with white latex paint. Let dry.
3. Paint a second coat of white on the edges of the legs. Let dry.
4. Paint the steps chartreuse. Let dry.
5. Paint the inner sides pale pink.
6. Paint the outer sides fuchsia.
7. Using a #12 shader, paint black horizontal stripes on the edges, spacing them evenly to create the look of checks. Let dry.

3
Design Painting

1. Using the pattern provided, trace and transfer "Don't" to the top step and "Bug Me" to the lower step or, using a pencil, lightly print the words freehand. Paint lettering black, using a #1 script liner. Let dry.
2. Using the patterns provided, trace and transfer various bugs to the steps of the stool. Paint them using the colors listed. See "Tips for Painting Bugs." Let dry.
3. Outline bugs with black, using a #1 script liner. Let dry.

4
Finishing

Apply two to three coats waterbase varnish. Let dry between coats. ✎

Artist's Tips for Painting Bugs

- Make them bright and colorful.

- Use blue metallic paint on the wings to add shimmer and shine.

- Add fun, tiny details with a permanent marker. Make ants by adding tiny legs to three tiny balls. Paint centipedes with a fine line of paint and lots of legs. Add a spider web somewhere.

- Thin paints with water to create a wash of color - almost a watercolor effect.

Closeup of stool - instructions on page 48.

*The following bug patterns are used for "Don't Bug Me" stool, pictured on page 49;
"Time Out" chair, pictured on page 55; and
"Stop Bugging Me" shelf, pictured on page 56.*

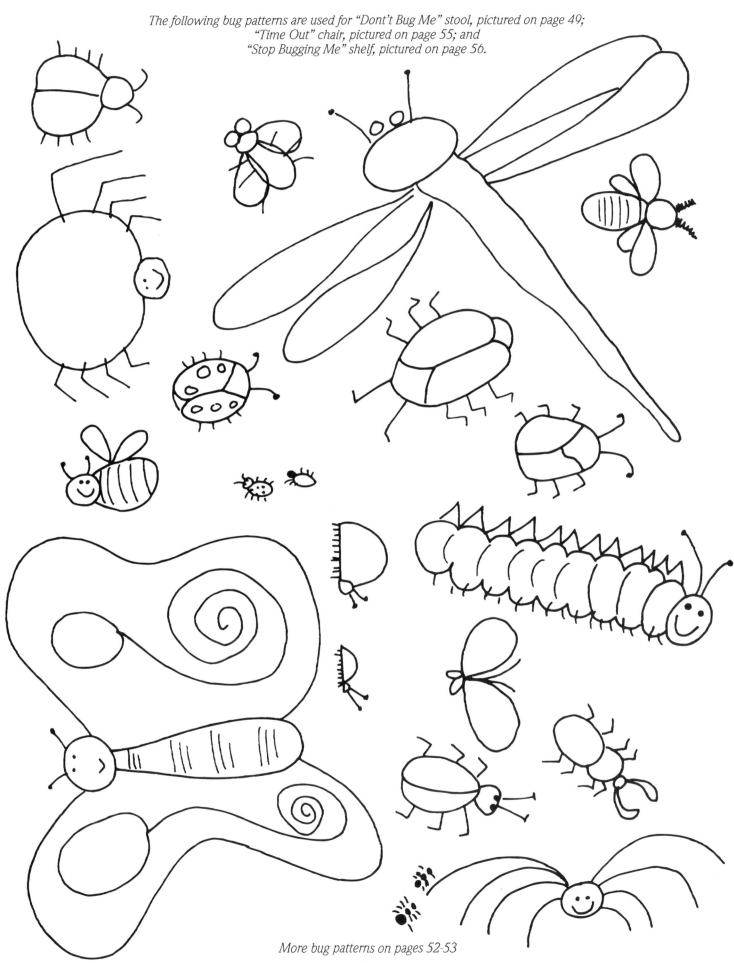

More bug patterns on pages 52-53

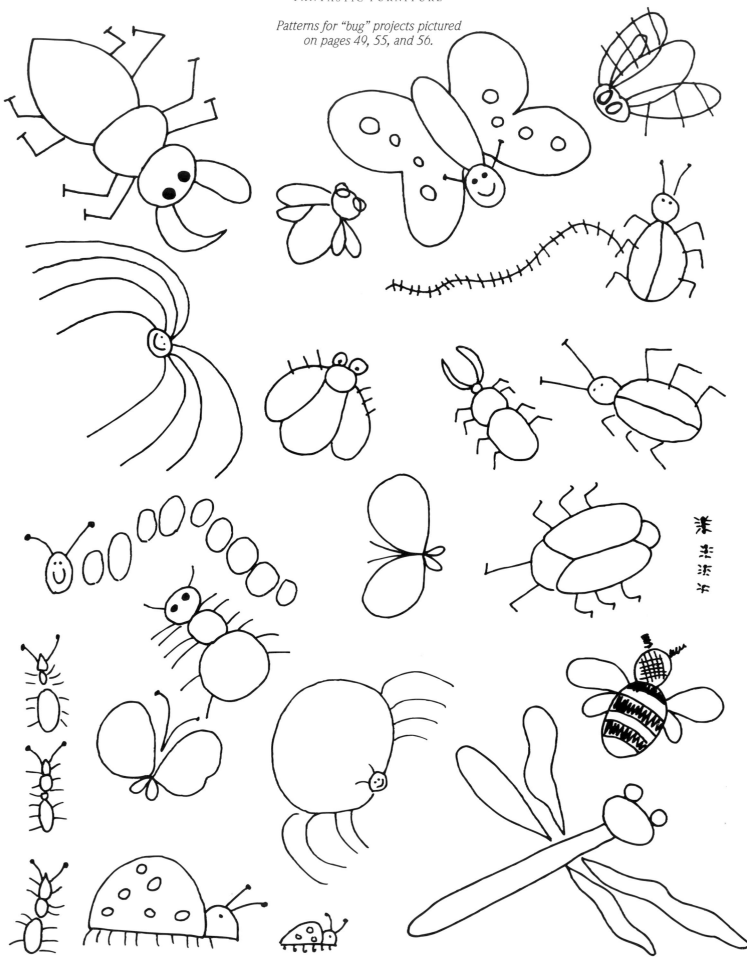

*Patterns for "bug" projects pictured
on pages 49, 55, and 56.*

Patterns for projects pictured on pages 49, 55, and 56.

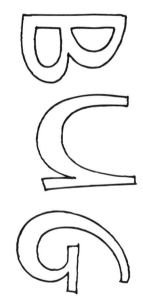

DON'T BUG ME

TIME OUT

Stop bugging me

You're bugging me!

TIME OUT

handpainted child's chair

Here's the perfect chair for "time out" times—painted with bright colors and decorated with black and white checks and a collection of colorful bugs. A child wouldn't mind "time out" at all. You can use the patterns provided or try writing the lettering in your own freehand. Write the letters on tracing paper and hold the paper over the chair to see if you like how they look.

Created by Allison Stilwell

1
Supplies

Furniture Piece:
Child's rustic chair with woven straw seat

Latex wall paint, eggshell finish:
White, 8 oz. is enough

Acrylic Craft Paints:
Aqua
Black
Blue (metallic)
French blue
Fuchsia
Green
Orange
Lime green
Peach
Purple
Yellow

Artist's Paint Brushes:
Shaders - #4, #8
Script liner - #1

Other Supplies:
Tracing paper
Transfer paper & stylus
1" sponge brush
Waterbase varnish
Sandpaper, fine grit
Masking tape, 1/2" wide

2
Preparation & Base Painting

1. Lightly sand chair to remove any rough spots. Wipe away dust.
2. Base paint the wooden parts of the chair with white latex paint, being careful not to get paint on the seat. Let dry.
3. Mask off 1/2" stripes on tops of chair backs, at the tops and bottoms of legs, along the top edge of the back leg stretcher, and around the left leg. See photo for placement.
4. Paint front and back legs lime. Let dry.
5. Paint back French blue.
6. Paint front and right leg stretchers aqua.
7. Paint left and back leg stretchers peach. Let dry.
8. Remove tape. Using a #4 shader, paint vertical stripes with black on white horizontal stripes for a checkerboard effect. Let dry.

3
Design Painting

1. Using the patterns provided, trace and transfer "Time Out" to the chair back and "You're Bugging Me" on the front leg stretcher or lightly write the lettering freehand, using a pencil. Paint the lettering black, using a #1 script liner. Let dry.
2. Using the patterns provided, trace and transfer various bugs to the legs, stretchers, and back of the chair. Paint them using the colors listed. See "Tips for Painting Bugs." Let dry.
3. Outline bugs with black, using a #1 script liner. Let dry.

4
Finishing

Apply two to three coats waterbase varnish to the wooden parts of the chair. Let dry between coats. ⤐

See pages 51 - 53 for project patterns.

STOP BUGGING ME

handpainted shelf

This wall shelf with a message is painted with pastels and decorated with bright bugs and a black and white checked edge. It's the perfect place to use colorful flower pots as storage containers.

Created by Allison Stilwell

Supplies

Furniture Piece:
Wooden wall shelf with scalloped base

Latex wall paint, eggshell finish:
Warm white, 8 oz. is enough

Acrylic Craft Paints:
Aqua
Black
Blue (metallic)
Bright blue
Chartreuse
Fuchsia
Green
Orange
Pale peach
Peach
Purple
Yellow

Artist's Paint Brushes:
Flat - 3/4"
Script liner - #1

Other Supplies:
Tracing paper
Transfer paper & stylus
1" sponge brush
Waterbase varnish
Sandpaper, fine grit

See pages 51 - 53 for project patterns.

56

2
Preparation & Base Painting

1. Lightly sand the shelf. Wipe away dust.
2. Base paint with warm white latex paint. Let dry.
3. Paint the top and edge of the shelf with a second coat of warm white. Let dry.
4. Paint the underside of the shelf chartreuse.
5. Paint scalloped shelf base pale peach.
6. Paint the edge of the scalloped base peach.
7. Using a 3/4" flat brush, paint vertical black stripes on the edge of the shelf for a checkerboard effect. Let dry.

3
Design Painting

1. Using the pattern provided, trace and transfer "Stop Bugging Me" to the scalloped base or print freehand, using photo as a guide for placement. Paint lettering black, using a #1 script liner. Let dry.
2. Using the patterns provided, trace and transfer various bugs to the scalloped base. Paint them using the colors listed. See "Tips for Painting Bugs." Let dry.
3. Outline bugs with black, using a #1 script liner. Let dry.

4
Finishing

Apply two to three coats waterbase varnish. Let dry between coats. ❧

LUSCIOUS LEMONS

magazine table

The simple oval shapes of lemons and leaves adorn the sides of this magazine table. The table top has a distressed finish that adds the look of character and age. It was created by applying layers of paint and sanding the edges of the table to reveal the different colors and some of the bare wood underneath.

Created by Allison Stilwell & Tracy Page Stilwell

1
Supplies

Furniture Piece:
Wooden magazine table

Latex wall paint, eggshell finish:
Off white, 1 pint is enough

Acrylic Craft Paints:
Burnt umber
Chartreuse
Green
Lavender
Mint green
Yellow

Artist's Paint Brushes:
Flats - 3/4", 1/2"

Tools & Other Supplies:
Foam brush
Sandpaper, fine and medium grits
Matte spray sealer

See page 60 for project patterns.

2
Preparation & Base Painting

1. Prepare table for painting, following the instructions in the "Furniture Preparation" section.
2. Base paint the table with off white latex paint. Let dry. Sand. Wipe away dust. Paint a second coat of off white. Sand again. Wipe away dust. Add a third coat if necessary for opaque coverage.

3
Painting the Colors

Legs:
1. Paint the insides and outsides of the legs chartreuse. Let dry.
2. Paint the edges of the legs with lavender. Let dry.
3. Using a 3/4" flat brush, paint green horizontal stripes on edges of legs for a checkerboard effect.

Lower Shelf:
1. Paint the top of the shelf and the edges lavender.
2. Paint the bottom of the shelf mint green.

Table Top:
1. Loosely paint the edges of the table top with burnt umber. (This will be painted over, so you can just slap it on.) Let dry.
2. Cover the dark brown with a coat of mint green. Let dry.
3. Cover the mint green with a coat of chartreuse. Let dry.
4. With a 1/2" brush, paint green vertical stripes on the edges of the table top. Let dry.
5. Paint the table top—but not the edges—with another coat of off white. Let dry completely.

4
Distressing

See "About Distressing" (page 60).
Using fine and medium sandpaper, sand the top and top edges of the table, giving more attention to the edges. Sand to expose all the layers of paint—and, in some places, the bare wood—to create an aged look. Wipe away dust.

5
Painting the Lemons

You can paint the lemons using the pattern on page 60 or paint them freehand, following the instructions on page 60. Use the pattern supplied for the leaves or lightly draw simple ones with a pencil and fill them in.
1. With a 1/2" flat brush, paint the lemons with yellow.
2. Paint the leaves with green. Let dry completely.

6
Finishing

Spray with matte sealer.

LEMONS

About Distressing

Distressed finishes add the character imparted by use and age to a piece of furniture. You can create a simple distressed finish by painting a piece with layers of color and sanding after the paint has dried. This removes some of the paint, exposing layers of color and allowing some of the wood to show. Sand more on the edges of the piece—concentrating your efforts in places where wear would normally occur over time—and less on flat areas for a more natural appearance.

For this type of sanding, don't use a sanding block or an electric sander—you want an uneven look. Holding the sandpaper in your hand is best and allows you more control. Use medium or medium-fine grit sandpaper to remove more paint, fine grit sandpaper to remove less. It's best to begin slowly and err on the side of removing too little paint rather than too much. You can always sand again to remove more. Stop when the result pleases you. After sanding, use a tack cloth to wipe away dust. ❧

How to Paint a Lemon

The lemons can be painted with a transferred pattern or freehand, using a 1/2" flat brush with a mixture of yellow and golden yellow. To paint them freehand, follow these simple steps. Practice on a piece of poster board or heavy paper before painting on your project.

1. Paint a curved stroke on one side.
2. Paint an opposite curved stroke for the other side to create an oval shape.
3. Paint a small oval shape on the blossom end (the bottom end, opposite the leaves).
4. Fill in the larger shape a bit on each end. ❧

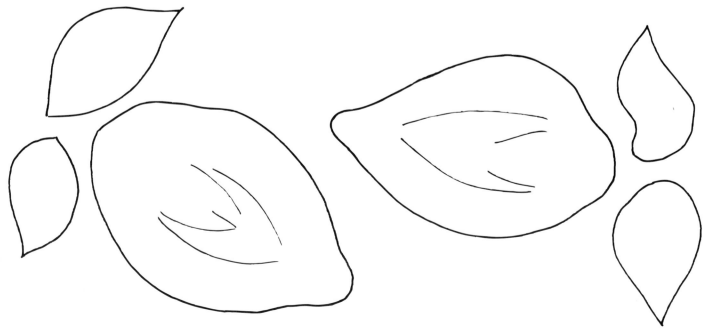

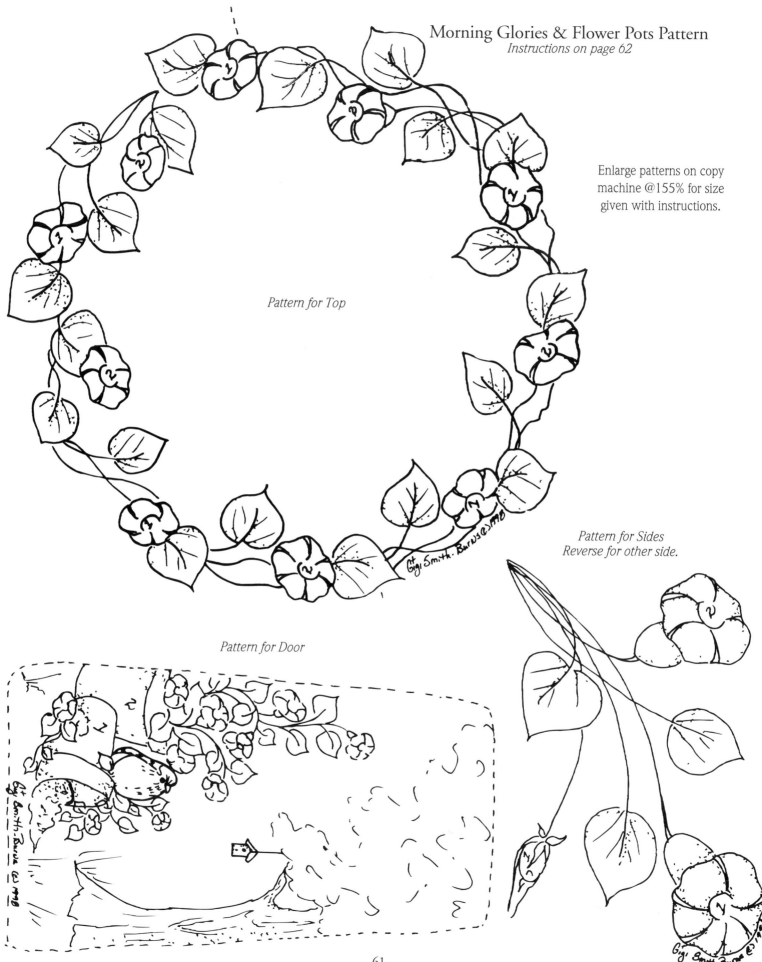

Morning Glories & Flower Pots Pattern
Instructions on page 62

Enlarge patterns on copy
machine @155% for size
given with instructions.

Pattern for Top

*Pattern for Sides
Reverse for other side.*

Pattern for Door

MORNING GLORIES & FLOWER POTS

plant stand with decorative painting

Morning glories bloom all day long on the top and sides of this plant stand and in the garden scene that's painted on the door of the storage compartment under the top. Step-by-step instructions for painting morning glories and leaves are found on the Painting Worksheet, "How to Paint Morning Glories."

Created by Gigi Smith-Burns

1
Supplies

Furniture Piece:
Wooden plant stand

Latex wall paint, eggshell finish:
Warm white, 1 pint is enough

Acrylic Craft Paints:

Black	Deep black green
Fuchsia	Golden brown
Golden tan	Indigo
Lavender	Pale blue gray
Pale gray	Pale yellow
Purple	Warm white
White	

Acrylic Artist's Paints:

Green umber	Light red oxide
Burnt umber	Green light
Green medium	Green dark

Artist's Paint Brushes:
Angle - 1/2"
Script liner - #0
Deerfoot
Flat wash - 1"
Scruffy brush or old toothbrush for spattering

Tools & Other Supplies:
Extender acrylic painting medium
Tracing paper
Transfer paper & stylus
Wet palette
Eraser
Waterbase varnish

2
Preparation & Base Painting

1. Remove door pull, hinges, latch, and door. Prepare the plant stand for painting, following the instructions in the "Furniture Preparation" section.
2. Base paint the plant stand, door, and latch with warm white latex paint. Let dry. Apply a second coat. Let dry. Apply a third coat, if needed to achieve complete coverage.
3. Trace the design and enlarge as needed to fit your plant stand. Transfer lightly.
4. Moisten the door with extender. Slip-slap pale gray in the lower left and upper right corners. Place warm white + a touch of pale yellow in the center to indicate sunlight.

3
Design Painting

NOTE: Use a 1/2" angle brush for most shading and highlighting. Use extender in your brush, but not a lot—blot the brush after dipping it in the extender. The brush is side-loaded unless indicated otherwise.

Standing Flower Pot:
1. Basecoat with light red oxide.
2. Shade with burnt umber.
3. Highlight with light red oxide + a touch of warm white.

Tipped Over Flower Pot:
1. Basecoat with a mix of one part light red oxide + two parts warm white.
2. Shade with light red oxide.
3. Highlight with warm white + a touch of light red oxide.
4. Reinforce shading with light red oxide + burnt umber.
5. Paint soil falling out of flower pot with golden brown and burnt umber.

Leaves:
1. Randomly basecoat leaves with various colors, using green light, green medium, and green medium + green dark. Use photo as a guide for color placement. Let dry.
2. Apply extender over entire area; then, using a large brush with extender in it, pick up green umber and wash over design area to provide the back shading under the design. Let dry.
3. On green light leaves, shade with green umber and highlight with pale yellow.
4. On green medium leaves, shade with deep black green and highlight with pale yellow.
5. On green medium + green dark leaves, highlight with pale yellow.
6. Add veins to all leaves and loosely outline with deep black green. Paint vines with deep black green.

Continued on page 64

continued from page 62

Deep Pink Morning Glories:

1. Basecoat with fuchsia.
2. Shade with fuchsia + a touch of indigo.
3. Apply veins with pale blue gray. Shade on either side of veins with shading mix (fuchsia + a touch of indigo).
4. Sideload with warm white and paint the throat. Let dry. Repeat with pale yellow.

Purple Morning Glories:

1. Basecoat with lavender.
2. Shade with purple.
3. Apply veins with pale blue gray. Shade on either side of veins with purple + a touch of indigo.
4. Sideload with warm white and paint the throat. Let dry. Repeat with pale yellow.

Bird:

1. Base body with pale gray. Shade with indigo. Highlight with white.
2. Paint head with black. Streak with white.
3. Paint wing with pale gray. Streak with burnt umber.
4. Shade bird's body with indigo. Reinforce shading with black.
5. Paint eye black. Highlight with warm white.
6. Paint beak pale yellow. Shade with golden tan.

Tree:

1. Wash trunk with golden brown. Shade with burnt umber. Reinforce shading with deep black green.
2. Using a deerfoot brush, stipple the foliage with green light, green medium, and green dark + a touch of deep black green.

Birdhouse:

1. Basecoat walls with pale gray. Shade with indigo.
2. Paint roof with light red oxide.
3. Outline and paint entrance holes and wire with black.

Filler Flowers and Grass:

1. Load a liner brush with warm white. Paint petals.
2. Dot centers with pale yellow.
3. Pull up blades of grass with deep black green, using a liner brush. Let dry.

Closeup of door

4
Finishing

1. Install hinges, door, and latch.
2. Spatter with indigo and fuchsia. Wipe spatters off hinges with a cotton swab. Let dry completely.
3. Apply two or more coats waterbase varnish. Let dry between coats.
4. Install door pull. ❧

How to Paint Morning Glories
Painting Worksheet

Fig. 1: Flowers and leaves are basecoated and shading is applied.

Fig. 2: Shading is reinforced on leaves and veins are added on flower petals.

Fig. 3: Leaves are highlighted. Flowers are shaded on either side of each vein. Throats of flowers are painted and highlighted.

Fig. 4: Shading is reinforced on flowers. Leaves are loosely outlined.

Painting Terms from Gigi Smith-Burns

Shade: To darken or deepen an area; normally placed where an object turns or goes under something. Sometimes I use several layers of shading, with each successive layer stopping short of the previous layer. The object is to lead the eye to the deepest area.

Highlight: To lighten or brighten an area; makes an area appear closer or brighter. I use both first and second highlights. The first highlight is usually done with a duller, yet light color. Second highlighting is done with a brighter color.

Pivot Highlight: Sometimes called the pivot cheek technique, the pivot highlight puts color in a circular area. Sideload a flat or angle brush with the color specified. With the color to the inside, pivot the brush in a circle, keeping the water edge to the outside.

Shimmer: Floated color on an area, with the outside fading out and the center the brightest area. Using a sideloaded brush that has been softened on the palette, float color, then quickly reverse the process by flipping the brush and floating color against the color that was placed first. This creates a shimmer effect with a bright center and faded outer edges.

Sideload: Using a flat brush or an angle brush, load one side of the brush with color. Do not allow the paint to travel across more than 1/4 of the bristles; blend brush on a wet palette.

DRAGONFLIES & DAISIES

stamped & stenciled tea table

Stenciled daisies and stamped dragonflies decorate this colorful tea table. Outlining the design is easy with a permanent black marker. Stenciled checks form a border on the table top and adorn the tops of the legs. Patterns are provided for cutting the stencils. What a bright spot this would be in a sun room.

Created by Kathi Malarchuk

1
Supplies

Furniture Piece:
Wooden table

Latex wall paint, eggshell finish:
Yellow, 1 pint is enough

Acrylic Craft Paint:

Black	Green
Lavender	Magenta
Purple	White

Tools & Other Supplies:
Pre-cut stamp - dragonfly design
Stencil blank material
Craft knife
Medium tip black permanent marker
Masking tape
Stencil brushes
Sponge brushes
Small sponge roller
Sandpaper, fine grit
Waterbase varnish

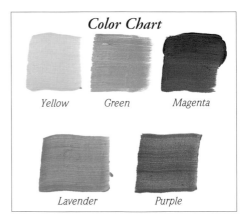

Color Chart

Yellow Green Magenta

Lavender Purple

Instructions follow on page 68

continued from page 66

2
Preparation & Base Painting

1. Prepare the table for painting, following the instructions in the "Furniture Preparation" section.
2. Base paint the table top and legs with two coats yellow latex paint. Let dry and sand between coats.
3. Base paint the table apron with two coats lavender. Let dry and sand between coats.

3
Stenciling the Daisies

1. Trace daisy patterns on stencil blank material. Cut out with a craft knife.
2. Stencil front petals (the smaller ones) with white on table apron, using photo as a guide for placement. Stencil centers with magenta.
3. Mask off a 1 3/4" area on table top where the checked border will be stenciled.
4. Using photo as a guide for placement, randomly stencil back flower petals (the larger ones) on table top (**photo 1**). Use magenta for some and lavender for others, overlapping in some areas. Let dry.
5. Stencil front flower petals over lower flower petals, using lavender over the magenta ones and purple over the lavender ones. See photo for color placement. Let dry.
6. Stencil flower centers with white. Let dry.
7. Outline the flowers with a medium tip black marker (**photo 2**).

4
Stamping the Dragonflies

1. Load the center of the stamp (the dragonfly's head, thorax, and tail) with black paint. Load the wings with green paint (**photo 3**).
2. Holding the stamp by its handle, place stamp on surface and press gently and carefully with your fingers to make a print (**photo 4**). Use the handle to lift the stamp from the surface (**photo 5**). Stamp the rest of the dragonflies, using the same technique and colors. To make it appear as though part of the dragonfly is under the daisy, tape over the daisy before stamping.
3. Remove tape from border area. Let paint dry completely.

5
Checked Borders

1. Trace checkerboard pattern on stencil blank material. Cut out with a craft knife.
2. Stencil checks with green around edge of table top and on tops of legs. Use photo as a guide for placement. Let dry completely.
3. Outline the checked border on the table top with the black marker. Use a straight edge to help you get an straight and even line.

Photo 1. *Stencil larger daisy petals first, using a stencil brush.*

Photo 2. *Outline the flowers with a black marker after stenciling.*

Photo 3. *Holding the stamp by its handle, load the stamp with paint, using a small sponge roller or sponge brush.*

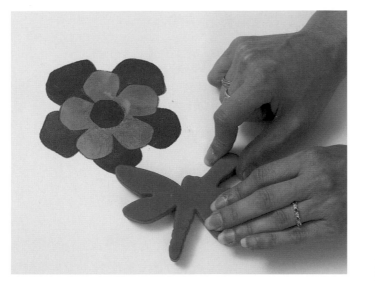

Photo 4. *Press the stamp on the surface, pressing gently and evenly with your fingers to achieve a good print.*

Photo 5. *Lift the stamp by the handle without sliding the stamp on the surface.*

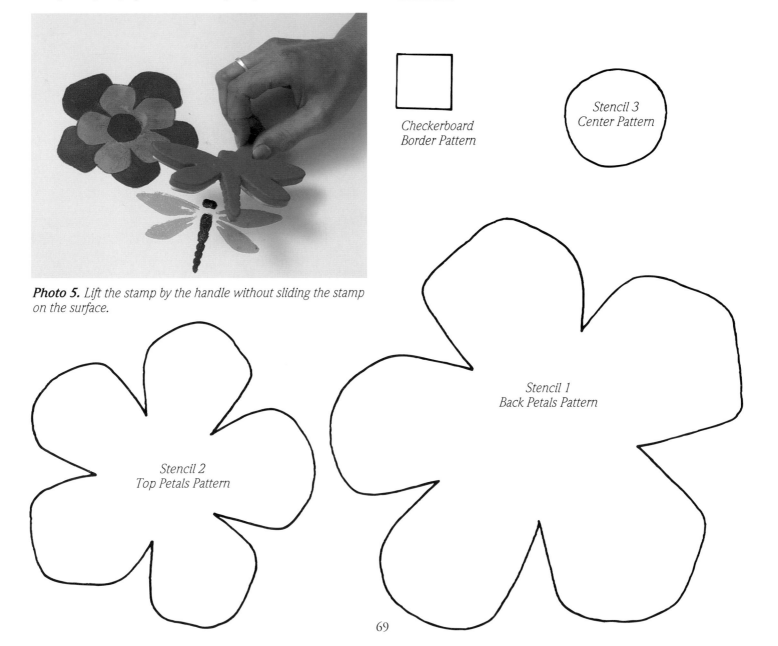

Checkerboard Border Pattern

Stencil 3 Center Pattern

Stencil 1 Back Petals Pattern

Stencil 2 Top Petals Pattern

6
Striping

1. Mask off stripes 1" wide on table legs, using photo as a guide for placement.
2. Paint stripes with purple and lavender. See photo for color placement. Remove tape. Let dry.
3. Paint edge of table top with purple. Let dry.

7
Finishing

Seal with two to three coats waterbase varnish. Let dry between coats. ❧

STAR QUALITY

handpainted bentwood chair

Tropical colors enhanced with transparent colored glazes make something special of a simple bentwood chair. The colors are contrasted with crisp black and white—dots on the curved leg stretchers and a border of checks around the seat. Simple golden stars are handpainted on the seat and the inner curved part of the chair back with metallic paint.

Created by Allison Stilwell & Tracy Page Stilwell

1
Supplies

Furniture Piece:
Bentwood chair

Acrylic Craft Paint:
Aqua
Black
Fuchsia
Gold (metallic)
Lavender
Violet
White

Artist's Paint Brushes:
Flats - 3/4", 1/2", 1/4"
Small round brush

Tools & Other Supplies:
1" or 2" foam brush
Sandpaper, fine grit
Pencil
Tack cloth
Glazing medium - neutral
Matte sealer spray

Color Chart

Violet   Fuchsia   Gold

Aqua   Lavender

2
Preparation & Base Painting

1. Prepare the chair for painting and prime, following the instructions in the "Furniture Preparation" section.
2. Paint the legs and the back with one to two coats violet. Use as many coats as needed for opaque coverage. Let dry and sand lightly between coats.
3. Paint the seat with one to two coats aqua.
4. Paint the rim of the seat with one to two coats lavender. Let dry.
5. Paint the curved support stretchers under the seat with black. Let dry.

3
Glazing

*When mixing glazes, use three parts neutral glazing medium and one part paint (**photo 1**). The colored glaze will add a veil of color, but the base paint color should be visible. Use the 3/4" glaze brush or a foam brush to apply the colored glaze (**photo 2**).*

1. Mix neutral glazing medium and fuchsia. Brush over legs and outer part of chair back.
2. Mix neutral glazing medium and pale aqua. Brush over inner part of chair back. Let dry.
3. Mix neutral glazing medium and gold metallic. Brush randomly here and there on inner part of chair back.

4
Painting the Details

1. With a pencil, lightly draw triangles around the rim of the seat. Use photo as a guide. Paint the triangles aqua.
2. Using a small round brush, paint white dots on the curved support under the seat. Use a generous dip of paint to make each dot.
3. Using a 1/2" brush, paint a white band the width of the brush around the outer edge of the chair seat. Let dry.
4. Using a 1/4" brush, paint two rows of black checks on the white band, alternating the checks to form a checkerboard. Let dry.
5. Trace and transfer the star patterns to the seat. Paint with gold metallic. *Option:* Paint the stars freehand.
6. Draw smaller stars with a pencil on the seat among the larger stars and on the inner part of the chair back. Paint them with gold metallic. *Option:* Paint the small stars freehand. Let dry completely.

5
Finishing

Spray with matte sealer. ❧

See page 72 for how-to photos and patterns.

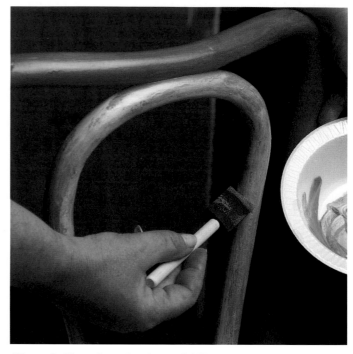

Photo 1. *In a disposable foam bowl or a jar, mix three parts neutral glazing medium and one part paint. Stir to blend completely.*

Photo 2. *Use a foam brush or a 3/4" glaze brush to brush the glaze mixture on the surface.*

Pattern for Stars

Closeup of chair seat

HAPPINESS & JOY

stenciled & glazed chair

Created as a birthday gift, this armchair was painted with bright colors and accented with colored transparent glazes. Stenciled letters form inspirational messages for the recipient ("happiness" and "joy"). Stamped symbols (a sun and a heart) and spirals, squiggles, and stars further personalize a special gift.

Created by Allison Stilwell & Tracy Page Stilwell

1
Supplies

Furniture Piece:
Wooden chair with arms and slat back

Acrylic Craft Paint:
Aqua, 4 oz.
Black
Bright blue
Lime green, 4 oz.
Orange, 4 oz.
Golden yellow, 4 oz.
Violet, 4 oz.
White
Fuchsia

Artist's Paint Brushes:
Flats - 3/4", 1/2", 1/4"

Tools & Other Supplies:
Sandpaper, fine grit
Tack cloth
Primer
1" or 2" foam brush
Alphabet stencil, 1" letters
Pre-cut stamps - 3/4" heart, 2-1/2" sun
Glazing medium - neutral
Fine tip black permanent marker
Matte sealer spray

2
Preparation

1. Prepare the chair for painting, following the instructions in the "Furniture Preparation" section.
2. Prime chair, following instructions in "Furniture Preparation" section. Sand lightly. Wipe away dust.

3
Base Painting

All base painting and design painting is done with the acrylic craft paint which is usually sold in 2 oz. size. You will need two bottles of the colors used for base painting. Apply as many coats of the base colors as needed to obtain opaque coverage. Let dry between coats.

1. Paint the arms, legs, and seat apron with violet.
2. Paint the seat aqua.
3. Paint the top and bottom back pieces golden yellow.
4. Paint the vertical back pieces lime green.
5. Paint the top edge of the top back piece orange.

4
Glazing

When mixing glazes, use three parts neutral glazing medium and one part paint. The colored glaze will add a veil of color, but the base paint color should be visible. Use the 3/4" glaze brush or a foam brush to apply the colored glaze.

1. Mix neutral glazing medium and fuchsia. Apply to sections of front legs and seat apron. See photo for color placement.
2. Mix neutral glazing medium and bright blue. Apply to seat.
3. Mix neutral glazing medium and orange. Apply to top and bottom back pieces. Let dry completely.

5
Adding Details

1. Using a 1/4" brush, paint a horizontal white stripe along the bottom of the top back piece and the top of the bottom back piece. Let dry.
2. Using the same brush, paint black checks on the white stripes. Let dry.
3. Paint black accents to turned areas of front legs. See photo for placement.
4. Paint white accents where the front legs are turned to become the arm supports. See photo. Let dry.
5. Using a fine tip black marker, add squiggles, spirals, dots, triangles and stars—or any shape that pleases you—to the edges of the arm rests and the white-painted trim.
6. Stamp the sun with golden yellow on the front of the chair apron.
7. Use alphabet stencil to stencil inspirational words with orange (we used "Joy," "Happiness") on the yellow areas of the back.
8. Stamp a heart with orange above the lettering on the top. Let dry completely.

6
Finishing

Spray with several coats matte sealer. Let dry between coats. ❧

ROSES FROM YESTERYEAR

handpainted chair

Before refinishing and decorating a special find, Ginger Edwards spends time studying the piece and contemplating the various ideas that come to mind. This chair was once painted white, but the finish had peeled badly. Ginger really liked the look of the flaked paint and decided not to strip it off. Instead, she smoothed the remaining paint and accented it with soft, elegant roses. If you can't find an interesting old chair, choose an unfinished one and apply a white wash to it.

Created by Ginger Edwards

1
Supplies

Furniture Piece:
Wooden spindle back chair

Acrylic Craft Paints:
Chartreuse
Cream
Deep blue
Raspberry
Deep blue green
Golden yellow
Ivory
Rose pink
Teal green
White

Acrylic Artist's Paints:
Burnt umber
Burnt sienna
Sap green

Artist's Paint Brushes:
Flats - #20, #12, #10
Filbert - #8
Liner - #1

Acrylic Painting Mediums:
Floating medium
Blending medium

Other Supplies:
Stiff bristle brush (for cleaning chair)
Gray transfer paper & stylus
Waterbase varnish (brush-on)
Brown paper bag
Optional: Matte acrylic spray sealer, sandpaper

2
Preparation

1. Use a stiff bristle brush to brush away any loose flaking paint. Sand lightly, if necessary.
2. Wipe all surfaces of the chair with a damp cloth. Let dry.
3. *Optional:* If the wood on your chair is very old and porous, spray all surfaces with a light coat of matte acrylic sealer. Let dry.
4. Buff with a crumpled piece of a brown paper bag.
5. Trace the pattern. Enlarge or reduce on a copy machine as needed to fit your chair. Transfer the pattern, using gray transfer paper and a stylus.

3
Design Painting

See the Rose Painting Worksheet. Using blending medium to moisten the surfaces prior to painting and when adding layers of shading and highlighting will make blending easier.

Roses:

1. Base with rose pink. Sideload the brush into ivory to stroke the edges of the outer petals.
2. Shade with raspberry. Deepen shading with raspberry + a tiny amount of deep blue green.
3. Highlight with white + a tiny amount of cream.
4. Tint inside the throats of the roses with a tiny amount of golden yellow.
5. Stipple flower centers with burnt umber + a tiny amount of raspberry; thin the paint mixture with a bit of water for a softer appearance.
6. Using the liner brush and the same mixture, paint stamen around the stippled center. Tap the tips of the bristles to add a few splotches of color throughout the stamen.

Leaves and Buds:

1. Paint all leaves with teal green that has been thinned with water to a semi-transparent consistency.
2. Shade the leaves with sap green. Let dry and shade further with deep blue green + a tiny amount of burnt umber.
3. Highlight the leaves with chartreuse.
4. Paint the center veins in the leaves using a liner brush with chartreuse.
5. Paint the side veins with the shading mixture.
6. Paint the buds using the same colors for the roses and leaves.

Continued on page 78

Continued from page 76

Stems and Tendrils:

1. Paint the stems with thinned burnt umber. Let dry.
2. Shade the stems with burnt umber + a tiny amount of deep blue green.
3. Highlight with ivory + a tiny amount of burnt sienna.
4. Use the liner brush with burnt umber + a small amount of raspberry to paint a few thorns on the stems. Thin the paint to a semi-transparent consistency.
5. Paint tendrils with sap green + a small amount of deep blue.

Blossom Flowers:

After completing the roses, stems, and leaves, add a few blossoms to enhance the design. Keep these soft and indistinct so they don't overpower the roses. Complete each flower cluster before moving to the next.

1. Brush deep blue that has been thinned to a transparent consistency underneath where you will be painting the flowers. See the Painting Worksheet, Fig. 2. Brush the paint so that the edges of the area fades away.
2. Use a filbert brush to paint the flower petals with white + a small amount of deep blue violet. For the more prominent flowers, add a bit more white to your mixture. Let dry.
3. Add dots of cream to the centers of some flowers.

4
Finishing

1. Add washes of colors from the design to other parts of the chair, such as the turned legs or back spindles. Here, teal green was used on some areas, deep raspberry on others. Use the project photo as a guide for adapting the idea to your chair. Let dry.
2. Seal the chair with several coats of brush on waterbase varnish. ❧

How to Paint Roses
Painting Worksheet

Fig. 1: The rose is filled with color and the outer petals are established. The center back section has several layers of petals. Adding a small amount of acrylic blending medium to the paint allows the paint to stay wet longer and increases the amount of time you have for blending. Allow the paint to dry before proceeding.

Fig. 2: The front of the cup and additional petals have been painted near the outer petals. The paint is blended so there are no harsh edges of color inside the rose. In this illustration, you can also see the first shading on the leaves and bud and the underpainting for the blossom flowers.

Fig. 3: The few petals that complete the rose are stroked between the outer petals and the front of the cup. The shading and highlighting is completed. Leaves have been shaded, and highlights, tints, and veins have been added to them. Stems are shaded. The petals of the blossom flowers are stroked in, and dots of colors indicate their centers.

Enlarge pattern on copy machine @135%. Refer to photo for placement.

Roses from Yesteryear Painting Pattern

*Enlarge on copy machine @135% and
adjust the patterns to fit your chair.*

Closeup of chair seat

FERNS

Table & Chairs

A crisp green and white color scheme and a random stenciled design create a custom look on a round pedestal table and four ladderback chairs. The crackled table top is strewn with stenciled fern fronds in greens and golden browns. The same stencil and colors were used on white fabric to create a coordinating print for upholstering the chair seats.

Created by Kathi Malarchuk

1
Supplies

Furniture Pieces:
Round wooden table, 48" dia.
Wooden ladderback chairs with upholstered seats

Latex wall paint, eggshell finish:
White
Dark green

Stencil Paint Gels:
Dark green
Light green
Medium green
Russet brown

Tools & Other Supplies:
Crackle medium
Pre-cut stencil - fern fronds
Stencil brushes
Palette
Paint brushes
Waterbase varnish
Sandpaper, fine and extra fine grits
Tack cloth
White fabric (enough to cover chair seats)

Instructions follow on page 84

continued from page 82

2
Preparation & Base Painting

1. Prepare the table and chairs for painting, following the instructions in the "Furniture Preparation" section.
2. Base paint the table and chairs dark green. Let dry. Sand lightly with fine sandpaper. Wipe away dust. Apply a second coat of dark green. Let dry completely.
3. Wash and dry fabric for chair seats according to manufacturer's instructions. Press.

3
Crackling the Table Top

1. Apply crackle medium to the table top, following manufacturer's instructions. Let dry according to instructions.
2. Following crackle medium manufacturer's instructions, brush table top with white paint. Cracks will form as paint begins to dry. Let dry.

4
Stenciling

On the Table Top:
Stencil fern fronds on table top over crackling. Scatter the fronds randomly. Use all the stencil gel colors, blending and shading for variety. Let cure 48 hours.

On the Fabric:
1. Place a piece of extra fine sandpaper under the white fabric to keep it from slipping. Stencil fern fronds on fabric with stencil gels, using the same random placement as used on the table top. Let dry 24 hours.
2. Heat set with a dry iron, using a pressing cloth.

5
Finishing

1. Seal table and chairs with waterbase varnish. Apply several coats to table top to protect it. Let dry between coats.
2. Cover chair seats with stenciled fabric. ❧

Closeup of table top

SUNNY ORCHARD

striped & stamped cupboard

This cupboard has painted stripes, a sunburst painted on its curved top, and a door that's decorated with stamped fruit. The lettering around the door is a quote from the American poet Walt Whitman: "Give me the splendid silent sun with all his beams full dazzling/Give me juicy autumnal fruit ripe and red from the orchard."

Created by Kathi Malarchuk

1
Supplies

Furniture Piece:
Wooden cupboard with curved top

Latex wall paint, eggshell finish:
Ecru
White

Indoor/Outdoor Acrylic Paints:
These were purchased in 8 oz. size.
Cherry red
Olive
Pale aqua
Purple
Red
Yellow

Artist's Paint Brushes:
Flats, #8, 10
Round, #6,10
Liner, #0

Tools & Other Supplies:
Foam stamps - sun, pears, grapes, cherries, apples
Stencil blank material
Craft knife
Fine tip black permanent marker
Medium tip black permanent marker
Masking tape
Measuring tape
Chalk
Sponge brushes
Waterbase varnish
Ruler or straight edge

2
Preparation & Base Painting

1. Remove door. Remove hinges and door pull. Prepare the cupboard for painting, following the instructions in the "Furniture Preparation" section.
2. Base paint cupboard (not door) with two coats of ecru wall paint. Let dry and sand between coats.
3. Base paint door with two coats of white.
4. Base paint door pull with cherry red acrylic craft paint.
5. Spray hinges and screws with matte sealer. Let dry. Paint hinges and screw heads with ecru.

3
Painting the Stripes

1. Mark off stripes 2" wide on the sides and front of the cabinet, using a pencil and ruler. Apply masking tape to the outsides of each stripe you will be painting. You will need to mask and paint one stripe at a time. Allow paint to dry before removing tape, then position tape for the next stripe.
2. Paint the stripes on the sides, working from back to the front and alternating the colors. Leave the first stripe ecru (the background color), then paint next stripe with purple, pale aqua, and cherry. Repeat the color rotation.
3. Paint the two sets of stripes on the front as shown with cherry and purple, leaving the center stripe in the set the ecru background color. Paint the rest of the front, except the curved top, with pale aqua paint. Let dry. Remove all tape.

4
Painting the Door

1. Mask off a border 2-3/4" wide on the cupboard, around the door. Paint white. Let dry. Remove tape.
2. Trace pattern for checks on stencil blank material. Cut out stencil with a craft knife.
3. Position stencil on door. Stencil checks with ecru.

5
Stamping

1. Fruit designs are stamped randomly on the door. Apply paint to stamps with sponge brushes, using olive for leaves and stems and these colors:
   Apples - cherry red, apple blossoms - yellow
   Pears - yellow, pear blossoms - cherry
   Grapes - purple
   Cherries - cherry, cherry blossoms - yellow.

Continued on page 88

continued from page 86

2. Stamp sun in corners of white border of cabinet with yellow, using photo as a guide for placement. Let the stamp bleed off the edges of the border on some corners. See photo.

3. Stamp the sun randomly on the sides with yellow, using photo as a guide for placement.

6
Painting the Top

1. Trace the sunburst pattern and transfer to the curved top of the cabinet.
2. Paint the background with white.
3. Paint the inner part of the sun with yellow.
4. Paint the middle sunburst and squiggles with red.
5. Paint s-shapes with purple.
6. Add dots with cherry.
7. Paint the top curved edge purple. Let dry.

7
Lettering & Outlining

1. Trace the pattern for lettering and transfer to the white border around the door.
2. Use black marker to write the lettering, outline the border on the door, and outline the sun on the curved top. Use a ruler or straight edge to make the long lines.
3. Outline the stamped suns on the sides. Let dry thoroughly. ❧

Enlarge pattern for lettering @400% or use as a guide to letter freehand.

Closeup of cabinet front.

give me the splendid silent sun with all his beams full dazzling give me juicy autumnal fruit ripe and red from the orchard

Patterns for Cupboard

Enlarge on copy machine @110%

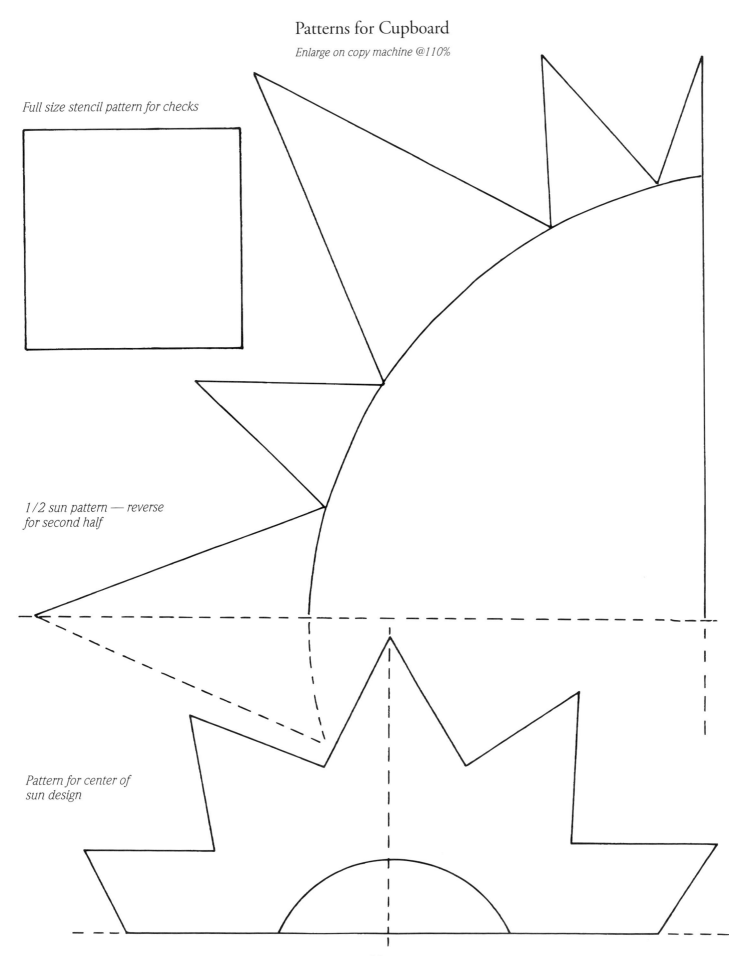

Full size stencil pattern for checks

1/2 sun pattern — reverse for second half

Pattern for center of sun design

DOTS & STRIPES

easy painted chair

A captain's chair becomes a fun accent piece when it's painted with bright colors. Because most chairs of this sort have different details, use the photo as a guide for painting and adapt the design and instructions to fit your chair.

Created by Allison Stilwell & Tracy Page Stilwell

1
Supplies

Furniture Piece:
Wooden captain's chair

Latex wall paint, eggshell finish:
Cream color

Acrylic Craft Paint:
Black
Yellow
Green
Hot pink
Light green
Pale aqua
Pale pink
Periwinkle
Turquoise
White
Violet

Artist's Paint Brushes:
Flats - 1/2", 3/4"
Round - #1
Script liner - #1

Tools & Other Supplies:
1" or 2" foam brush
Sandpaper, fine grit
Tack cloth
Matte sealer spray

2
Preparation & Base Painting

1. Prepare the chair for painting, following the instructions in the "Furniture Preparation" section.
2. Base paint the chair with cream latex paint, using a foam brush. Let dry. Sand. Wipe away dust.
3. Paint the seat and the outer leg stretchers with a second coat of cream paint. Let dry.

3
Adding the Colors

1. Paint the arm piece and the back stretcher black.
2. Paint the top of the back and the largest area of the thin spindles pale pink.
3. Paint various parts of the legs, front stretcher, and spindles with yellow, hot pink, light green, pale aqua, pale pink, violet, and turquoise. Use as many coats as necessary to achieve sufficient coverage. Let dry.

4
Decorating

Decorate the various painted areas with painted stripes, checks, white dots, green vines, and periwinkle flowers. Let all paint dry completely.

5
Finishing

Spray with matte sealer. ✍

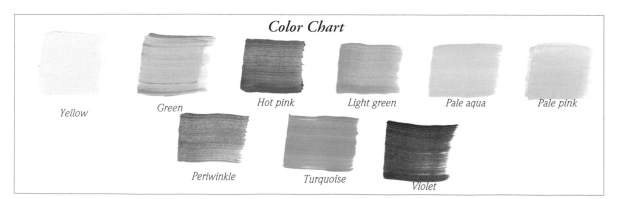

Color Chart

Yellow   Green   Hot pink   Light green   Pale aqua   Pale pink

Periwinkle   Turquoise   Violet

Decorating the Dots & Stripes Chair

Checks: *To paint checks, make short lines using a 1/4" or 1/2" flat brush with periwinkle. Alternate the placement of the painted lines to form the checked effect.*

Stripes: *Paint thin vertical stripes over the pale golden yellow parts of the chair with light green, using a #1 round brush.*

Dots: *Paint white dots on black areas, using a #1 round brush.*

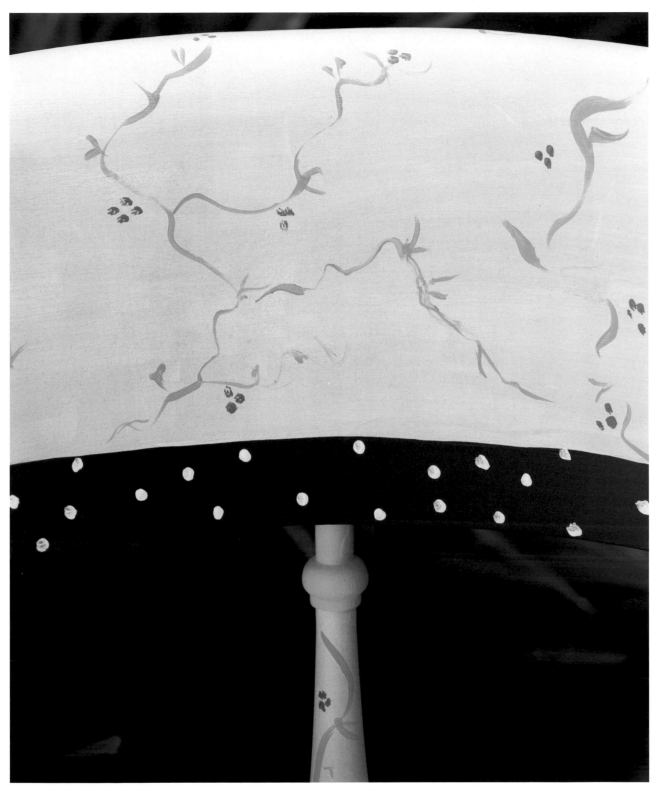

Vines & Flowers: *Paint green vines and leaves on pale pink parts of the chair. Paint the vines using a #1 script liner. Paint the leaves with a #1 round brush. Paint dot flowers randomly along the vines, using a #1 round brush with periwinkle. See the Painting Worksheet, "How to Paint Posies, Leaves & Vines."*

Sample pattern

SOUTHERN MAGNOLIAS

handpainted armoire

This armoire originally had a dark wood stain. The mirror in the door was broken and, rather than replace it, Chris Stokes has installed a piece of birch plywood as a panel in the door. As a background for the painted magnolia design on the door panel, Chris used a piece of purchased-by-the-yard lace as a stencil. The magnolia design on the panel also could be used over windows, to create a matching headboard for a bed, or on a dresser.

Created by Chris Stokes

1
Supplies

Furniture Piece:
Wooden armoire with a door on one side
    door and drawers on the other side

Latex wall paint, eggshell finish:
    Off white

Acrylic Craft Paints:
    Deep blue green
    Deep blue
    Raspberry
    Gold metallic
    Gray green
    Yellow ochre
    Ivory
    Warm white

Artist's Paint Brushes:
Flat glaze - 3/4"
Flat - #10
Liner - #10/0
Angle brush - 3/8"

Tools & Other Supplies:
Stencil brushes - 1/8", 3/8", 1"
Large natural sea sponge
Medium-size paint roller
Acrylic blending medium
Lace fabric, 5' long, 18" wide (large enough
    to cover the door panel)
Spray stencil adhesive
Sandpaper, 220 grit
Masking tape
Paper towels
Old toothbrush (for spattering)
Gold spray paint
Soft cloth rags
Waterbase varnish

2
Preparation & Base Painting

1. Remove drawer pulls and door hardware. Prepare the armoire for painting, following the instructions in the "Furniture Preparation" section.
2. Dampen sea sponge and squeeze out excess water. Load with waterbase varnish and off white latex paint. Pounce the paint-and-varnish mixture over the surface. Let dry.
3. Using a roller, roll the surface with off white latex paint. A textured look is achieved with this method, and many surface imperfections are covered. Let dry.

3
Stenciling the Door Panel

1. Spray one side of lace fabric with stencil adhesive. Press lace, adhesive side down, on door panel.
2. Load a 1" stencil brush with gray green. Blot brush on a paper towel. Pounce paint over lace. Let dry. Remove lace.

4
Sponging

1. Trace pattern outline for sponged areas on drawer fronts. Enlarge or alter as needed to fit your furniture piece. Transfer outline to surface.
2. Mask off around outline. Dampen a natural sponge. Pick up deep blue green, gray green, and blending medium on the sponge. Pounce over the drawer fronts, keeping outer perimeter darker. Re-load sponge as needed.
3. Mask off around top surface of armoire above the drawers. Re-load the sponge with the same colors. Sponge the top of the armoire. Let dry. Remove all tape.

5
Design Painting

See the "How to Paint Magnolias" Painting Worksheet.
Background:
1. Load a 1" stencil brush with deep blue green, raspberry, and yellow ochre. Pounce the brush on palette to blend. Pounce lightly on the areas where the magnolia designs will be painted—the door panel, the top corners of the top drawer, and the bottom corners of the bottom drawer. Keep this light and airy. Let dry.
2. Trace and transfer magnolia designs to door panel and drawer fronts.

Leaves:
The upper leaves are lighter than the background leaves, giving a dimensional look.
1. Thin mixes of raspberry, deep blue green, and yellow ochre with water until they are the consistency of ink ("inky"). Using a 3/4" glaze brush, paint the background leaves. Let dry.

Continued on page 96

continued from page 94

2. Using the same brush loaded with deep blue green and touches of yellow ochre and raspberry, paint the leaves, wiggling the brush on the surface. Pick up warm white for highlights.
3. Paint turned edges of leaves with a brush sideloaded with raspberry + a touch of yellow ochre.
4. Detail leaves with inky gray green.

Magnolia Blossoms & Buds:

Magnolias have nine petals in three layers. The three bottom petals are large, the next three are medium-sized, and the three on top are smaller.

1. Double load a 3/4" glaze brush with warm white and gray green. Wiggle in three lower petals.
2. Sideload a #10 flat with ivory and paint turned edges of petals.
3. Paint second layer of petals with same colors, picking up touches of raspberry and yellow ochre on your brush.
4. Repeat for the third (upper) layer of petals.
5. Load short end of 3/8" angle brush with deep blue green and raspberry. Load long end with yellow ochre. Pounce centers.
6. Using a liner brush, pull up fine "hairs" with warm white and yellow ochre.
7. Shade centers with floats of gray green.

Grapes & Grapevines:

This is Chris' quick and easy method for painting grapes. She uses a 1/8" stencil brush for small grapes and a 3/8" stencil brush for large grapes.

1. Double load brush with deep 1/2 raspberry and 1/2 yellow ochre + a touch of warm white. Pounce to blend colors. Place brush flat on painting surface and twist, keeping the lighter color on the left. This makes one red grape.
2. For another grape color, load brush with deep blue and warm white + a touch of raspberry. Repeat technique. Make a bunch of grapes, varying colors.
3. Paint twigs and tendrils, using a liner brush with inky mixes of deep blue green, raspberry, and yellow ochre. Let dry.

6
Painting the Trim

Drawer Pulls:
1. Paint wooden drawer pulls with deep blue green. Let dry.
2. Mist drawer pulls with gold spray paint. Let dry.
3. Install drawer pulls.

Top & Bottom Trims:
1. Dampen top trim with water. Paint with deep blue green. While paint is wet, wipe with a damp cloth to remove most of the paint. (Paint will remain in the crevices.)
2. Repeat on bottom trim. Let dry.

7
Finishing

1. Spatter entire piece with inky metallic gold. Let dry.
2. Reinstall door hardware.
3. Apply two to three coats waterbase varnish. Let dry between coats. ॐ

How to Paint Magnolias
Painting Worksheet

Fig. 1 - Background and background leaves: Areas where the magnolia designs will be painted are lightly pounced with deep blue green, deep raspberry, and harvest gold. Background leaves are painted with inky mixes of deep raspberry, deep blue green, and harvest gold.

Fig. 2 - Lower Petals: Larger lower petals are wiggled in with warm white and gray green. Turned edges of petals are painted using a brush sideloaded with ivory.

2a: Turned edge of petal.

2b: Petal before turned edge.

Fig. 3 - Second Layer of Petals: The same colors (warm white and gray green) with added touches of deep raspberry and harvest gold are used to paint the second layer of petals.

Fig. 4 - Third Layer of Petals: The upper petals in the third layer are the same colors as the second layer, but are smaller.

Fig. 5 - Flower Center: Centers are pounced using a 3/8" angle brush loaded on the short end with deep blue green and deep raspberry and loaded on the long end with harvest gold. Fine "hairs" are pulled up using a liner brush. Centers are shaded with floats of gray green.

Fig. 6 - Completed Flower with Leaves: Leaf is wiggled in with deep blue green + touches of harvest gold + deep raspberry. Turned edges of leaves are painted with deep raspberry + a touch of harvest gold.

Fig. 7 - Grapes: Stencil brushes double loaded with deep raspberry and harvest gold + a touch of warm white are positioned on surface with the lighter color on the left, then twisted to paint grapes. Then the brush is loaded with deep blue violet and the process is repeated. Twigs and tendrils are painted using a liner brush with inky mixes of deep blue green, deep raspberry, and harvest gold.

See patterns and closeup photo on page 98 - 99.

1

2 *2a* *2b*

5

3 *4*

7

6

*Outline for
sponged area.
1/4 patter.*

*Pattern for Drawer Fronts
Enlarge on copy machine @205% —
reverse for each corner.*

*Pattern for Door Panel
Enlarge on copy machine @235%.*

Closeup of door panel

STRAWBERRIES & CHECKS

handpainted table & chairs

Fun and colorful, a checked tablecloth with a border of strawberries is painted on this old drop leaf table. Clusters of strawberries are painted on the lace trimmed seat pads on the chairs. Chris Stokes says that seeing her strawberries growing in their strawberry pots inspired these designs.

Created by Chris Stokes

1
Supplies

Furniture Pieces:
Wooden drop leaf table
Wooden chairs

Latex wall paint, eggshell finish:
Off white

Acrylic Craft Paints:

Burgundy	Cherry
Burnt umber	Dark green
Golden yellow	Gray green
Yellow ochre	Light beige
Warm beige	Warm red
Warm white	

Artist's Paint Brushes:
Flats - #10
Glaze - 3/4"
Liner
Round - #3

Tools & Other Supplies:
Stencil brushes - 1", 5/8", 3/8"
3" sponge brush
Old toothbrush (for spattering)
Masking tape, 3/4"
Sandpaper, fine grit
Paper towels
Spray polyurethane, satin finish
Brush on polyurethane, satin finish

Continued on page 102

Table — Before

continued from page 100

2
Preparation & Base Painting

1. Prepare the table and chairs for painting, following the instructions in the "Furniture Preparation" section.
2. Base paint the table and chairs with off white, using a 3" sponge brush. Let dry.
3. Using masking tape, outline the tablecloth area on the table and the seat pad areas on the chairs. Using a 1" stencil brush, pounce these areas with warm white. Let dry thoroughly.

3
Painting the Tablecloth Checks & Border

1. Using masking tape, mask off a 2" border on all sides of the tablecloth.
2. With tape, mask off stripes in one direction. Paint with warm red + a touch of cherry, using a 1" stencil brush. As you paint, blot excess paint from the brush on a paper towel. Let dry completely. Remove tape.
3. Mask off stripes in the opposite direction to make checks. Paint with warm red + a bit more cherry, using a 1" stencil brush. Let dry. Remove tape.
4. Thin burgundy paint with water until the paint is the consistency of ink ("inky"). Using a 3/4" glaze brush, stroke where the stripes overlap.
5. Paint four-dot flowers with warm white on the lighter-colored checks. See photo.
6. Paint a thin band to border checked area with inky dark green.

4
Painting the Strawberry Designs

Vines & Background Leaves:
1. Paint the vines with inky dark green + a touch of dark brown, using a #3 round brush.
2. Using a #10 flat brush, paint background leaves with inky dark green + a touch of warm red. (After the strawberries are painted, more leaves will be added.)

Berries:
The berries are painted using a 5/8" stencil brush with various combinations of colors that are double loaded on the brush: yellow

Closeup of chair seat

ochre and burgundy, warm red and golden yellow, and cherry and burgundy. The technique is the same for each berry.
1. Double load brush. Pounce on palette to blend. Touch brush to surface and wiggle to form the berry.
2. Shade with burgundy.
3. Paint seeds with inky burnt umber + a touch of burgundy, using a liner brush. Highlight with warm white + a touch of golden yellow.

Foreground Leaves:
1. Double load #10 flat brush with deep green + a touch of burgundy. Paint leaves. Add touches of yellow ochre and warm white for realism.
2. Paint veins with inky gray green.

Blossoms & Tendrils:
1. Double load a 3/8" stencil brush with yellow ochre and dark green. Pounce centers. Pick up a bit of warm white to highlight.
2. Double load a #10 flat with warm white and yellow ochre + a touch of warm red. Paint petals.
3. Paint tendrils using a liner brush with inky burnt umber+ a touch of dark green.

5
Adding Details

1. Float shading at edges of tablecloth and seat pads with warm beige, using a 3/4" glaze brush. Let dry.
2. Paint the lacy edging on the tablecloth and seat pads with comma strokes of warm white.
3. Paint stitch marks around edges of tablecloth with cherry, using a liner brush.

6
Finishing

1. Paint sections of the table legs and chair legs with inky warm beige + a touch of light beige. Use the same color mix to paint the tops of the chair backs.
2. Paint bands on legs with inky warm red and inky dark green. Let dry completely.
3. Apply several coats brush-on polyurethane on tabletop and chair seats. Let dry between coats.
4. Spray legs, chair spindles, and chair backs with spray polyurethane. Use the same brand you used for the brush on finish for compatibility. ✎

Patterns

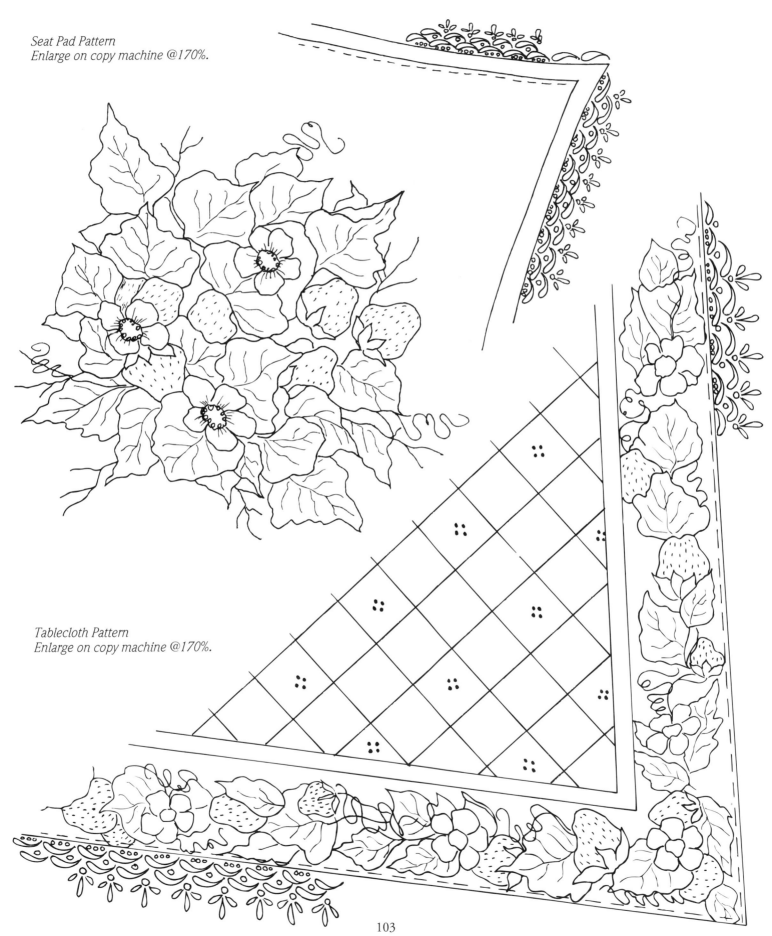

Seat Pad Pattern
Enlarge on copy machine @170%.

Tablecloth Pattern
Enlarge on copy machine @170%.

FORGET-ME-NOT

easel-top writing desk

*Ginger Edwards found her inspiration for the design for this desk in a book titled **Friendship's Token**, published many years ago by Cupples & Leon Co. The poem she lettered around the writing surface is attributed to Odie: "Friendship above all ties does bind the heart/And faith in friendship is the noblest part/If thou require a soothing friend/ Forget-me-not, forget-me-not." What better way to keep in touch with faraway friends, Ginger thought, than at a pretty writing desk?*

Created by Ginger Edwards

1
Supplies

Furniture Piece:
Wooden writing table with easel top and
   leather writing surface

Latex wall paint, eggshell finish:
Pale blue gray

Acrylic Craft Paints:
   Blue gray
   Cream
   Deep blue green
   Deep blue
   Dark green
   Golden yellow
   Light beige
   Pale yellow
   Periwinkle
   Warm white
   White

Acrylic Artist's Paints:
   Burnt sienna
   Burnt umber
Colored paint glaze - teal
Glazing medium - neutral

Artist's Paint Brushes:
Flats - 1", #14, #10, #4, #1
Filberts - #6, #4
Liner - 6/0
Mop Brush

Acrylic Painting Mediums:
Blending medium
Floating medium

Other Supplies:
Sandpaper, fine grit
Tack cloth
White primer spray
Transfer paper & stylus
Soft cloth rags (for wiping glaze)
Faux leather tool OR chamois and twine
   (see note below)
Masking tape
Pencil with soft lead
Fine tip brown permanent marker
Waterbase varnish

NOTE: You can make a faux leather tool with two 6" squares of chamois. Place one on top of the other, then gather at the center to make a tent. Tie twine tightly around the tip of the tent. The "leather" pattern is created by pressing the tool on wet glaze.

Writing Desk — Before

continued on page 106

continued from page 104

2
Preparation & Base Painting

1. Prepare the desk for painting, following the instructions in the "Furniture Preparation" section.
2. Mask off hinges to protect them from paint. Spray the piece with white primer. Let dry. Sand lightly. Wipe with a tack cloth.
3. Base paint the desk with pale blue gray. Use two coats for smooth, opaque coverage. Let the paint dry between coats

3
Glazing

1. Mix one part teal colored paint glaze with two parts neutral glazing medium. Brush glaze mixture on one small area of the wooden part of the desk, such as a leg or one side. While glaze is still wet, wipe off almost all the glaze, using a soft cloth. The glaze will remain in crevices and dents.
   - Working on one small area at a time prevents the glaze from drying too quickly on the surface.
   - Use a mop brush for final blending.
2. Wet the faux leather tool with water and squeeze out excess. Brush a coat of the glaze mixture over the leather top. While the glaze is still wet, press a pattern in the wet glaze with the faux leather tool. As you use the tool, rinse it occasionally in water to remove excess glaze. Squeeze excess water from the tool before resuming. Let the glaze dry thoroughly.
3. Thin a small amount of teal colored paint glaze with water. Spatter all surfaces of the desk except the leather top. Let dry.

4
Painting the Floral Designs

The flowers and leaves are most easily painted by basecoating the various elements, then shading each, and finally highlighting all. Lightly moistening the surface with blending medium or water will aid in brushing and blending the paint. See the "How to Paint Daisies & Forget-Me-Nots" Painting Worksheet for step-by-step illustrations.

1. Trace the pattern and transfer the daisy design.
2. Basecoat the design elements:
   Leaves - light beige

Daisy petals - blue gray thinned with water to a transparent consistency
Daisy centers - golden yellow
Forget-me-nots - periwinkle thinned with water to a transparent consistency.
3. Paint the stems with dark green + a small amount of deep blue green. Let dry.
4. Stroke transparent warm white on the daisy petals. Stroke periwinkle + a touch of white on the forget-me-nots.
5. Shade the design elements:
   Leaves - dark green
   Forget-me-not petals - periwinkle
   Daisy centers - burnt sienna
   Daisy petals - burnt umber + a tiny bit of deep blue green. Notice that the side and back petals are shaded next to the center, while the tips of the front petals are shaded.
6. Deepen the shading:
   Leaves - deep blue green + a small amount of deep blue
   Daisy centers - burnt sienna + burnt umber
   Forget-me-not petals - deep blue.
7. If necessary, apply a second application of the shading mixture to the daisy petals.
8. Highlight the design elements:
   Leaves - cream + a small amount of dark green (The leaves may not need highlighting, since the light basecoat should be visible.)
   Forget-me-not flowers - periwinkle + a touch of white
   Daisy petals - white + a speck of cream
   Daisy centers - pale yellow.

5
Completing the Painting

1. Use cream to paint the light throats of the forget-me-nots; then add a dot of burnt sienna in each.
2. Paint the center veins in the leaves with cream + a tiny amount of dark green. Paint the side veins with deep blue green + a tiny amount of burnt umber.
3. Add dots of golden yellow around the daisy centers, then add lighter dots of pale yellow.
4. Use the tip of a brush handle and periwinkle to make the dots for the forget-me-not buds.
5. Paint indistinct leaves among the buds with dark green + a tiny bit of deep blue green. Let dry.

Continued on page 108

How to Paint Daisies & Forget-Me-Nots
Painting Worksheet

Fig. 1 - Basecoating: The leaves and daisy centers are basecoated with one coat of opaque paint. The daisy petals and forget-me-not petals are stroked with paint made semi-transparent with water. The stems are indicated with thinned paint. After painting, allow to dry.

Fig. 2a - First Shading: This left side of the illustration shows the first shading on the leaves, daisy center, and forget-me-nots. The daisy petals are stroked with transparent paint, allowing the base paint to show through.

Fig. 2b - Second Shading: This right side of the illustration shows the deeper shading on the leaves. The daisy petals are shaded near the center on the side and on the outer edges of the front petals.

Fig. 3 - Completed Design: The shading on the daisy center, leaves, and forget-me-nots is deepened. Throats of the forget-me-nots are painted. Highlights are stroked on the daisy petals and pollen dots are painted. (The left side of the illustration does not show the pollen dots so you can better see the dark triangles between the petals near the center.) Veins are added to the leaves. Dots of color to indicate forget-me-not buds are added to the stems. The background is added to the right side of the design.

The top border of this worksheet show a stippled border created with a colored glaze and a French brush. The side border shows how the glaze looks with a faux leather finish, created with a faux leather tool.

1

2a

2b

3

continued from page 106

6
Painting the Background

Lightly moisten the entire design and the surrounding area with neutral glazing medium and, using a large flat brush, add color to the background. Begin with blue gray, then add some deep blue, and finish with deep blue green + deep blue.

- Use a soft mop brush to aid the final blending.
- Add a bit of glazing medium to the paint as you pick it up with the brush.
- Use a brush dampened with water to remove any background color that accidentally may have been brushed on the flowers or leaves.

7
Finishing

1. Use a soft lead pencil to lightly write Odie's verse about friendship around the edge of the top.
2. When you're satisfied with the placement, use a brown fine tip marker to go over the letters.
3. Using a #1 flat brush, accent the letters first with thinned burnt umber, then with thinned blue gray.
4. Protect the desk with several coats of satin waterbase varnish. Let dry.
5. Remove tape from hinges. If your desk has metal hinges or supports that have become discolored with age, try buffing them with a piece of crumpled aluminum foil. This gives a mellow sheen without destroying the aged appearance. ❧

Pattern for Front of Desk (center)

Pattern for Corners

Closeup of writing desk

FORGET-ME-NOT

handpainted folding chair

This chair had resided in Ginger Edwards' attic for years. Once she decided on a design for her writing desk, she needed a pretty folding chair to go with it. The size of the chair was appropriate for the table, so she finished it to match.

Created by Ginger Edwards

1
Supplies

Furniture Piece:
Wooden folding chair

Latex wall paint, eggshell finish:
Pale blue gray

Acrylic Craft Paints:

Blue gray	Cream	Deep blue green
Deep blue	Dark green	Golden yellow
Light beige	Pale blue gray	Pale yellow
Periwinkle	Warm white	White

Acrylic Artist's Paints:
Burnt sienna   Burnt umber

Acrylic Painting Mediums:
Blending medium   Floating medium

Other:
Colored paint glaze - teal   Neautral glazing medium

Artist's Paint Brushes:
Flats - 1", #14, #10, #4, #1
Filberts - #6, #4
Liner - 6/0
Mop brush

Other Supplies:
Sandpaper, fine grit
Tack cloth
White primer spray
Transfer paper & stylus
Soft cloth rags (for wiping glaze)
French brush
Masking tape
Pencil with soft lead
Waterbase varnish

Instructions follow on page 112

Folding chair — Before

continued from page 110

2

Preparation &
Base Painting

1. Sand the chair to remove any existing finish, gloss, and loose particles. Wipe with a tack cloth.
2. Spray the chair with primer. Let dry. Sand the surface lightly.
3. Base paint the chair with pale blue gray latex paint. Two coats will be necessary for a smooth opaque coverage. Let the paint dry between coats.

Pattern for back of chair

3

Glazing

Two glazing techniques were used on this chair.

1. Mix one part teal colored paint glaze with two parts neutral glazing medium. Brush glaze mixture on one small area of the seat or back of the chair. While glaze is still wet, wipe off almost all the glaze, using a soft cloth. The glaze will remain in crevices and dents. Continue until the seat and back are complete.
   - Working on one small area at a time prevents the glaze from drying too quickly on the surface.
   - Use a mop brush for final blending.
2. On the legs and back supports, stipple glaze with a French brush. (This requires very little glaze.) Let the glaze dry thoroughly.
   - The glaze will dry a shade darker than it appears when wet.
   - If the color of the stippled finish is darker when dry than you expected, soften the color with a wash of pale blue gray.
3. Thin a small amount of blue gray paint with water. Spatter the chair. Let dry.

4

Painting the Floral Designs

The flowers and leaves are most easily painted by basecoating the various elements, then shading each, and finally highlighting all. Lightly moistening the surface with blending medium or water will aid in brushing and blending the paint. See the "How to Paint Daisies & Forget-Me-Nots" Painting Worksheet for step-by-step illustrations.

1. Trace the patterns and transfer the daisy designs.
2. Basecoat the design elements:
   Leaves - light beige
   Daisy petals - blue gray thinned with water to a transparent consistency
   Daisy centers - golden yellow

   Forget-me-nots - periwinkle thinned with water to a transparent consistency.
3. Paint the stems with dark green + a small amount of deep blue green. Let dry.
4. Stroke transparent warm white on the daisy petals. Stroke periwinkle + a touch of white on the forget-me-nots.
5. Shade the design elements:
   Leaves - dark green
   Forget-me-not petals - periwinkle
   Daisy centers - burnt sienna
   Daisy petals - burnt umber + a tiny bit of deep blue green. Notice that the side and back petals are shaded next to the center, while the tips of the front petals are shaded.

Continued on next page

Chair seat pattern — right corner; reverse for left

continued from page 112

6. Deepen the shading:
   Leaves - deep blue green + a small amount of deep blue
   Daisy centers - burnt sienna + burnt umber
   Forget-me-not petals - deep blue.
7. If necessary, apply a second application of the shading mixture to the daisy petals.
8. Highlight the design elements:
   Leaves - cream + a small amount of deep green (The leaves may not need highlighting, since the light basecoat should be visible.)
   Forget-me-not flowers - periwinkle + a touch of white
   Daisy petals - white + a speck of cream
   Daisy centers - pale yellow.

5
Completing the Painting

1. Use cream to paint the light throats of the forget-me-nots; then add a dot of burnt sienna in each.
2. Paint the center veins in the leaves with cream + a tiny amount of dark green. Paint the side veins with deep blue green + a tiny amount of burnt umber.
3. Add dots of golden yellow around the daisy centers, then add lighter dots of pale yellow.
4. Use the tip of a brush handle and periwinkle to make the dots that show the forget-me-not buds.
5. Paint indistinct leaves among the buds with dark green + a tiny bit of deep blue green. Let dry.

6
Painting the Background

Lightly moisten the entire design and the surrounding area with neutral glazing medium and use a large flat brush to add color to the background. Begin with blue gray, then add some deep blue, and finish with deep blue green + deep blue.

- Use a soft mop brush to aid the final blending.
- Add a bit of glazing medium to the paint as you pick it up with the brush.
- Use a brush dampened with water to remove any background color that may accidentally be brushed on the flowers or leaves.

Closeup of chair seat

7
Finishing

Protect the chair with several coats of satin waterbase varnish. Let dry between coats. ❧

WHITE ELEGANCE

distressed parlor table

This table is an example of how a plan can change. Ginger Edwards explains, "I sprayed this table with primer to prevent the old stain from bleeding through the new paint and asked my husband to sand the table lightly to smooth the finish when the paint was dry. He sanded more heavily than I had intended, exposing the wood in many places on the legs. I decided I liked how it looked, so I left the distressed look on the legs and apron and painted a design on the top."

Created by Ginger Edwards

1
Supplies

Furniture Piece:
Wooden table

Acrylic Craft Paints:
Deep blue green
Golden yellow
Ivory
Light beige
Mint green
Pale yellow
Warm white
White

Acrylic Artist's Paints:
Burnt sienna
Burnt umber
Payne's gray

Painting Mediums:
Blending medium
Floating medium

Artist's Paint Brushes:
Flats - #14, #12, #10
Liners - #1, #6/0
Mop brush

Tools & Other Supplies:
White spray primer
Transfer paper & stylus
Sandpaper, fine grit
Tack cloth

Pictured at right: Parlour table — Before

2
Preparation & Base Painting

1. Spray the table with a stain blocking primer. Let dry.
2. Sand to expose the bare wood in some places. Wipe with a tack cloth.
3. Paint the tabletop ivory for a smooth, opaque painting surface. Let dry.
4. Trace and transfer the pattern.

3
Design Painting

The painting will go faster if all elements of the design are basecoated, then shaded, and finally highlighted.

1. Basecoat the design elements:
   Leaves - light beige (One coat will give smooth, opaque coverage.)
   Flower petals - light beige next to the flower centers, warm white on the outer edges. Blend the paints while still wet. On the petals in front of the centers, apply warm white near the center and light beige on the outer edge. Blend as you did for the other petals.

Continued on page 116

114

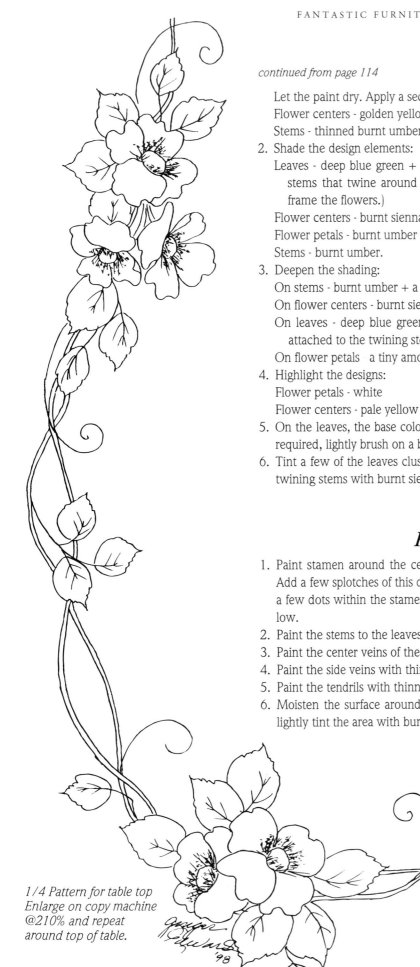

continued from page 114

Let the paint dry. Apply a second basecoat to the petals for a smooth opaque look.
Flower centers - golden yellow
Stems - thinned burnt umber.

2. Shade the design elements:
   Leaves - deep blue green + a tiny amount of burnt umber (The leaves attached to the stems that twine around the tabletop have much less shading than the leaves that frame the flowers.)
   Flower centers - burnt sienna
   Flower petals - burnt umber + a tiny amount of deep blue green
   Stems - burnt umber.

3. Deepen the shading:
   On stems - burnt umber + a tiny amount of Payne's gray
   On flower centers - burnt sienna + burnt umber
   On leaves - deep blue green + a tiny amount of Payne's gray (but not on the leaves attached to the twining stems)
   On flower petals   a tiny amount of Payne's gray.

4. Highlight the designs:
   Flower petals - white
   Flower centers - pale yellow

5. On the leaves, the base color shows through, creating highlights. If more highlights are required, lightly brush on a bit of mint green.

6. Tint a few of the leaves clustered around the flowers and all the leaves attached to the twining stems with burnt sienna.

4
Refining the Design

1. Paint stamen around the centers with burnt umber + a tiny amount of Payne's gray. Add a few splotches of this dark color with the tips of the bristles of the liner brush. Add a few dots within the stamen with golden yellow. Highlight with a few dots of pale yellow.

2. Paint the stems to the leaves with deep blue green + a tiny amount of burnt umber.

3. Paint the center veins of the leaves with mint green + a small amount of warm white.

4. Paint the side veins with thinned deep blue green + a tiny amount of burnt umber.

5. Paint the tendrils with thinned burnt umber.

6. Moisten the surface around the flower clusters with blending medium or water, then lightly tint the area with burnt umber to enhance the design. Let dry.

5
Finishing

1. Lightly spatter the tabletop with thinned burnt umber. Let dry.

2. Erase any visible pattern lines.

3. Brush on several coats of waterbase varnish. ❧

1/4 Pattern for table top
Enlarge on copy machine
@210% and repeat
around top of table.

How to Paint Wild Roses
Painting Worksheet

Fig. 1 - Basecoating: One coat of paint is used on the leaf and flower center. Two coats are used on the flower petals, and the two colors applied to petals are blended while wet. Allow to dry between coats. Allow the basecoats to dry before continuing.

Fig. 2 - First Shading: Shading is applied to the flower petals, flower center, leaf, and stem. Notice the shading on the side and back petals is next to the center, while shading is applied to the outer edge of the front petal. Lightly brush a small amount of blending medium over the surface to help blend the paint.

Fig. 3 - Shading & Highlights Completed: Shading is completed on the leaf, flower center, and stem. Highlights are brushed on the flower petals and tapped lightly on the center. Allow the previous step to dry and use blending medium to moisten the surface before deepening the shading or adding highlights.

Fig. 4 - Completed Design: Tints and splotches are added to the leaf. Veins are painted. Shading is deepened on the flower petals near the center. Light tints of color are added to some of the outer edges of the petals. The center of the flower is complete. A tendril and light spatters enhance the design.

Fig. 1

Fig. 2

Fig. 3

Fig. 4

Closeup of table top

RED ROSES ON BLUE

handpainted antique hutch

Simple handpainted roses adorn an antique hutch that's used to hold books, toys, and collectibles in a little girl's room. It would be equally at home in a breakfast room to hold dishes and cookbooks or in a hallway to hold crafts supplies, tools, or books.

Created by Stephanie Corder

1
Supplies

Furniture Piece:
Wooden hutch

Latex wall paint, eggshell finish:
Country blue, 1 gal.
Deep red, 1 gal.
Soft yellow, 1 qt.
Teal, 1 qt.
White, 1 qt.

Acrylic Craft Paint:
Gold metallic

Artist's Paint Brushes:
Flats - 3/4"
Round - #6
Liners - #1

Tools & Other Supplies:
White primer
Waterbase polyurethane, matte finish
China bristle paint brush, 4"
Tracing paper
Transfer paper & stylus
Masking tape
Sandpaper, medium and fine grits

Pictured at right: Closeup of hutch side.

Instructions follow on page 120

continued from page 118

2
Preparation

1. Prepare the hutch for painting, following the instructions in the "Furniture Preparation" section.
2. Apply primer to the entire piece. Let dry.

3
Painting the Inside

You may want to try out this wet-on-wet painting technique for creating the abstract roses on a piece of poster board before trying it on your hutch. Use the photo as a guide.

1. Paint the inside of the upper doors with deep red paint. Let dry.
2. Paint the shelves and the inner sides and back of the upper part of the hutch with deep red.
3. While the paint is still wet, use a round brush with white paint to make swirls on the red paint to create the abstract roses. (While you are painting them, they may seem too abstract; don't worry—after they dry, the effect will be good.) Let dry completely.

4
Painting the Outside

1. Mask off the painting on the inside with tape, pressing the edges for a good seal.
2. Paint the lower part of the hutch and the sides and front of the upper part with country blue. (Don't paint the glass-paned doors or the top surface of the lower part.) It may take more than one coat to completely cover the primer. Let dry between coats. Let final coat dry 24 hours.
3. Trace the design for the sides and transfer. Trace the design for the lower doors and transfer. (I usually paint the roses free hand with loose brush strokes. But you can transfer pattern if you feel more comfortable.)
4. Paint the roses with red paint, filling in the outlines with a 3/4" flat brush.
5. While the paint is still wet, use a round brush with white paint to outline, define, and highlight the petals within the shape.
6. Paint the lines that form the leaves, vines, and stems with teal. While still wet, add highlights with white.
7. Mask off the red paint on the inside of the glass-paned doors and mask off around the top of the lower part. Paint the frames of the glass-paned doors and the top of the lower part with yellow. Let dry. If needed, apply a second coat. Let dry.
8. Paint the edges of the wood that holds the glass panes with gold metallic. Using photo as a guide, paint diagonal gold stripes on the wood. Let dry.

5
Finishing

Apply three coats polyurethane finish with even strokes. Let dry three hours or more between coats. *NOTE: A matte finish is recommended because it adds to the richness of the color. With three coats, even a flat finish will develop a sheen.* ❧

Closeup of hutch inside back.

Patterns for Hutch

Enlarge on copy machine @135%.

ARTICHOKES & DELPHINIUMS

antique workbench

The rich, muted design of golden gourds, green and purple artichokes, and glorious blue delphiniums that adorns this wooden bench is reminiscent of a tapestry. The design could be adapted for a variety of furniture pieces.

Created by Stephanie Corder

1
Supplies

Furniture Piece:
Wooden bench

Acrylic Artist's Paints:
Burnt sienna
Cadmium medium yellow
Cadmium red deep
Cobalt green light
Dioxazine purple
Titanium white
Ultramarine blue

Latex wall paint, eggshell finish:
White (for primer)
Yellow ochre (or other neutral color), 1 qt.
Periwinkle, 1 qt.

Artist's Paint Brushes:
Flats - #14, #12, #10, 3/4"
Round - #4, #6
Liners - #1, #6/0

Tools & Other Supplies:
Paint brushes
Masking tape
Tracing paper
Transfer paper & stylus
Waterbase polyurethane, matte sheen

2
Preparation & Base Painting

1. Prepare the bench for painting and prime with white, following the instructions in the "Furniture Preparation" section. Let dry.
2. Paint the lower shelf with two coats periwinkle. Let dry between coats.
3. Paint the legs, shelf apron, and top with two coats ochre. Let dry between coats. Let final coat dry 24 hours.
4. Mask off a border 2" wide around the edge of the top. *TIP: Running your fingernail along the edge of the tape helps prevent the paint from bleeding under it.*
5. Mix some cadmium medium yellow with white wall paint to make a light yellow for the background of the painted design. Paint the area inside the tape with the light yellow mix. *TIP: Save some this color for any necessary touchups.* Let dry.
6. Trace pattern. Enlarge as needed. Transfer to center area of top, using photo as a guide.

Continued on page 124

continued from page 122

3
Design Painting

Gourds:

1. To cadmium medium yellow, add small amounts of dioxazine purple to mix a base color for the gourds. Add titanium white to some of the base color to create a highlight color.
2. Paint the gourds one at a time. First, basecoat with the base color, then go back over the outlines with dioxazine purple. To blend the lines, go back in with the base color to create a subtle shaded effect.
3. Blend a bit of burnt sienna with white. Add highlights along the edges of the gourds.
4. Paint the blossom ends with the highlight color.

Artichokes:

1. Add a touch of cadmium medium yellow and a touch of titanium white to cobalt green light to create the green for the artichokes. Add a little more cadmium medium yellow and titanium white to some of the green mix to create a highlight color.
2. Paint each leaf individually, highlighting as you go.
3. When the entire artichoke has been base painted and highlighted, add the shadows. The shadows are painted with the base color, dioxazine purple, cadmium red deep + dioxazine purple, and dioxazine purple + ultramarine blue.
4. With dioxazine purple, outline the bottom of each leaf. While the paint is still wet, randomly use the shadow colors to paint thin lines upward. *TIP: If your lines get too close together, paint over some of them with the base color and highlight color.*

Leaves:

Use the same colors and techniques to paint the abstract, curvy leaves. The leaves have a touch more blue and the same lining technique is used. *TIP: They're basically fun shapes, so have a good time with them. If your hand wants to go left instead of right, let it!*

Delphiniums:

Although the delphiniums may appear to be the most intricate part of the design, they are actually the simplest to paint. The freer your wrist, the more real they will appear.

1. Mix the base color with dioxazine purple + ultramarine blue. Add titanium white to some of the mix to create a highlight color.
2. Paint each flower individually, highlighting as you go. Slightly blend the colors between each flower to provide a sense of continuity.
3. Paint the flower centers with the highlight color.

Background Squiggles & Dots:

The squiggles and dots that make up the background provide pattern and movement and connect the various elements of the design. Have fun with them.

Paint squiggles and dots in background, using a liner brush with pale yellow (cadmium medium yellow + titanium white) and pale green (cobalt green light + cadmium medium yellow + titanium white). Let dry completely.

4
Finishing

Seal with three coats matte waterbase polyurethane. The three coats protect the painting. *NOTE: The slight sheen of the matte finish adds to the richness of the painting. A high gloss finish will diminish the effect of the painting, causing the color and detail to appear flat.* ❧

Enlarge pattern on copy machine @192%.

Closeup of bench top

METRIC CONVERSION CHART

INCHES TO MILLIMETERS AND CENTIMETERS

Inches	MM	CM
1/8	3	.3
1/4	6	.6
3/8	10	1.0
1/2	13	1.3
5/8	16	1.6
3/4	19	1.9
7/8	22	2.2
1	25	2.5
1-1/4	32	3.2
1-1/2	38	3.8
1-3/4	44	4.4
2	51	5.1
3	76	7.6
4	102	10.2
5	127	12.7
6	152	15.2
7	178	17.8
8	203	20.3
9	229	22.9
10	254	25.4
11	279	27.9
12	305	30.5

YARDS TO METERS

Yards	Meters
1/8	.11
1/4	.23
3/8	.34
1/2	.46
5/8	.57
3/4	.69
7/8	.80
1	.91
2	1.83
3	2.74
4	3.66
5	4.57
6	5.49
7	6.40
8	7.32
9	8.23
10	9.14

INDEX

Continued on next page

INDEX

Continued from page 127